THE SECRET TO A **HAPPY** AND **PROFITABLE**
HEALTH AND FITNESS BUSINESS

thrive
— DON'T JUST —
SURVIVE

KAREN INGRAM

RETHINK PRESS

First published in Great Britain 2017
by Rethink Press (www.rethinkpress.com)

© Copyright Karen Ingram

Cover image © Shutterstock / ESB Professional

Praise for
Thrive, Don't Just Survive

▼

'A must-read for every studio owner or movement professional who wants real measurable success. If you don't know where to start in analyzing your business, this book is for you. If you think you have a good business and plan but aren't sure, this book is for you. If you want to improve your business, this book is for you! Karen has created a simple, straight forward guide that illuminates the traps that mind body professionals fall into and how to avoid. "Thrive" takes the guesswork out of running a business and provides a solid action plan. So read, reflect and reap the reward!'

Zoey Trap
MS, Co-author of the Peak Pilates Instructor Certification and Team Leader.
Business mentor and owner of Pilates Solutions
www.pilatesstudiosolutions.com

'Excellent! A must-read for all health and fitness sector professionals, whether newly qualified or seasoned pros. As a highly successful business woman, Karen utilises her considerable experience, insight and talent to guide you step by step in building your own fulfilling, profitable business; steers you away from the common pitfalls of self-employment; and empowers you to achieve a healthy life/work balance.'

Dr Cate Davies
MBBS, Peak Pilates Level 1 Certified Instructor

'This book will resonate with every health professional running their own business – an incredibly valuable guide to achieve a thriving, healthy practice.'

Jane Spill
Nutritional Therapist

CONTENTS

Chapter eight

**PART THREE: SUSTAINING A HAPPY AND
PROFITABLE LIFESTYLE BUSINESS**

Chapter Nine

Introduction

Are you one of the many skilled therapists or fitness instructors who went into business to share your passion and help other people? Despite your passion and commitment, do you struggle to attract clients, earn a living wage and manage your time? Are you surviving, rather than thriving, in business? Despite being good at what they do, many people in the health, wellbeing and fitness sector struggle to earn a living wage. Some, at best, have a 'paying hobby' that just about covers the cost of their next course or qualification, while others make a loss, or are shored up by a second family income. The danger is to end up working long, often anti-social hours and catching up with admin late into the night whilst feeling over-worked, burnt out and hating the admin burden of being a sole trader. Hardly the dream lifestyle!

In *Thrive* I share the secret of how you can combine your talent and passion for what you do with simple and effective business tools to make being in business a joy. I outline some of the common pitfalls that therapists and fitness instructors fall prey to when starting out in business, and take you through five clear steps to get your business healthy, happy and fit.

So whether you are a Pilates or Yoga Teacher, Massage Therapist, Counsellor, Nutritional Therapist, Osteopath or Acupuncturist, you can learn the secret of running a profitable and happy lifestyle business from this book.

Who I am

Like many women in their mid-thirties, I switched careers from a salaried job to run my own wellness business, working as a Sole Trader. I went on to co-found Barefoot Studio, a Pilates and wellness space and over the last sixteen years have successfully grown the business into one of the UK's largest Pilates studios. As a Teacher Trainer I have certified hundreds of people to become Nordic Walking Instructors and Pilates Teachers and I've worked with many therapists, including Osteopaths, Counsellors, Nutritional Therapists, and Massage Therapists.

In my previous 'day job' I worked in homelessness, crime and disorder, in both the not-for-profit sector and local government, managing large teams, fundraising, and setting strategic direction. When I started working in Health and Fitness, I began to realise that many people ran their businesses as if they were not-for-profits, with no eye on the bottom line. In effect, they become misguided philanthropists.

I now run a Training Academy for Pilates teachers, which combines teacher training with business skills training. My passions for working to help other people and business have come together to enable others to share my success. I believe you can run a happy and profitable business and I want you to believe you can do it, too!

Who this book is for

If you are a Yoga or Pilates Teacher, a Complimentary Therapist, Counsellor, Osteopath, Massage Therapist, Acupuncturist, or Nutritional Therapist, then this book is for you. It is also for you if you are looking to change careers and move into the Health and Fitness sector or return to work having had children. Perhaps you have been a Sole Trader for a while and have struggled to make a decent wage and are looking for a new approach.

The method I have developed is applicable to any small business owner and I've used it to help re-focus everyone from Artists to Acupuncturists. Any business that grew from a personal passion will benefit from this approach. By following the simple steps outlined and changing your mindset, you can learn to thrive in business, not just survive.

How to use this book

This book is divided into three parts:

- Part One outlines some of the common pitfalls of running a Health and Fitness business.

- Part Two lays out clear steps to follow to change your business into a happy and profitable one as you work through the 5 Ms method.

- Part Three looks to the future and how to ensure your business is sustainable and enjoyable to run in the long term

You can read this book sequentially or dive into the sections that most interest you. Look out for the **DO! EXERCISE** sections. These are practical exercises to get you thinking like a business person, to work through a problem and to hone your product, pricing and planning. If you struggle to work through these on your own, then ask a friend or partner to help you. We are all far more creative in a group setting.

I encourage you to keep a journal as you work through this method. It will help clarify your thinking and will give you something to look back on six months from now to see how far you have progressed. You can use the notes to share with your 'Virtual Board' that we talk about in chapter nine.

Enjoy the journey!

PART ONE

Surviving
Not Thriving

'And once the storm is over you won't remember how you made it through, how you managed to survive. You won't even be sure, in fact, whether the storm is really over. But one thing is certain. When you come out of the storm you won't be the same person who walked in. That's what this storm's all about.'

Haruki Murakami
Japanese Author

Understanding the Problem

In the first part of *Thrive* I'm going to outline some of the common problems that many people experience when running a Health and Fitness business. We will look at some of the common myths and beliefs that people hold about being in business and begin to unpick them.

In the first chapter we look at values. You may see a conflict between delivering a service based on strong values and running a profitable business. We will explore this common misunderstanding and start to get you thinking like a business person.

In the second chapter I'm going to describe three types of business to avoid, the 'superhero', 'paying hobby' and 'busy but broke' business models. You may well identify with one – or a little bit of all three – of these business types.

Many Sole Traders work from home or in relative isolation and can suffer from 'lone worker syndrome'. In the third chapter we look at the reality of being your own boss and how it can make you feel.

The **DO! EXERCISE** at the end of Part One will give you a vital benchmark against which to measure your progress as you work through the *Thrive* model. It will enable you to measure success and know if your business is on the right track and reaching your goals.

By the end of Part One you should have a good understanding of the pitfalls and problems your business might face or maybe some of the mistakes you have already made. An honest appraisal of where you are starting from, sets you in exactly the right place to move forward.

CHAPTER ONE

A Business Based On Values Is Still a Business

▼

Like many entrepreneurs, people in the Health and Fitness sector are driven by their belief and passion for what they do. Many have a strong personal story of how their own life was turned around by the very thing they now practise professionally. I often say that Pilates saved my life, twice! First time around I was on the waiting list for a second back operation and in constant pain. After trying every therapy and treatment known to man, I eventually came across Pilates and my journey back to full health began. So profound was my own experience that I went on to give up my well-paid job to re-train as a Pilates Instructor and to start my own business. This was the second way Pilates saved my life, by getting me out from behind a desk and doing a job I love.

I desperately want to help as many people as possible who are experiencing chronic or acute back pain. My motivation for being in business is not to make my fortune, but to help other people. My company, Barefoot Studio, is based on very strong values, with the people we work with at its heart. However, it is still a profitable business.

Unfortunately, our passion for what we do can lead us to make poor business decisions. Many therapists and teachers have, in effect, become misguided philanthropists, holding a belief on some level that it is not morally right to profit from others' needs or problems.

Ask yourself the following five questions:

1. Have you ever worked with someone free of charge because their story affected you and it felt 'wrong' to charge?

2. Do you often allow people to cancel their appointments at the last minute without charging them because you felt it was not their fault they were in pain, or that they were struggling on that day?

3. Do you decide what to charge based on what you think people should/could pay rather than what would be profitable and fair for you?

4. Do you work reactively rather than with a clear plan for what you need to earn or by using goals and targets?

5. Do you spend as little time as possible on the business side of what you do, fire-fighting rather than working to a plan?

If you answered yes to two or more of these questions, then you are probably one of the many Therapists, Pilates, Yoga or Fitness teachers who don't perceive themselves to be in business. You are going to benefit massively from following the five-step method. Remember, when you earn a decent income you can afford to help more people, to book onto the latest professional development courses and, ultimately, to thrive.

When you earn a good income you can then choose to be philanthropic and offer a free or discounted service to those people who genuinely can't afford you and really need what you offer. You can't afford to do this when you are trading at a loss or just about breaking even.

Common Myths

These are all statements that people working in the heath and fitness sector have said to me over the years. They are all false beliefs:

- 'I'm really busy therefore I must be making money'
- 'If I was better qualified it'd be okay and I'd get more customers'
- 'As long as I have clients I will make money'
- 'If I pay for advertising/marketing I will definitely get more clients'
- 'The less I charge the more clients I will get'
- 'High prices will put off people in my area'
- 'I need to bend over backwards to accommodate my clients or they will go elsewhere'
- 'Charging a lot for what I do is immoral, people need help and it's not their fault'
- 'I can't enforce a cancellation policy, people only cancel at the last minute for genuine reasons'
- 'If someone is vulnerable they shouldn't have to pay for the thing that will make them well'
- 'I need to be bigger and better than all my competitors'
- 'It's only me, so I don't need ways other than cash to take payment'
- 'I can't sell a course or block of treatments. It's too pushy'
- 'I'm not making enough money from what I'm doing

currently, so the best idea is to diversify and add another string to my bow'

Let's look at three types of business model to avoid.

CHAPTER TWO

Three Types of Business to Avoid

▼

I have come to recognise three common types of business that people operate. You may recognise some of these traits in yourself, or in people you know. Many of us are a little bit of each.

The 'superhero' business

This is the therapist or teacher who spends all their time 'saving' others with no concern for their own survival. They give and give and give, both emotionally and financially. They will go out of their way to accommodate people. They undercharge or waive charges. They have no cancellation policy. They will run courses or sessions even when there are very low numbers and it makes no financial sense. They are a sucker for a sob story and feel bad charging people. This person has often been 'saved' by what they now practise and are evangelical about their discipline.

The 'paying hobby' business

This is the therapist or teacher who earns just enough money to cover the costs of their next training course or workshop with their favourite Yoga Guru or for that bit of equipment they've always wanted. They study a lot and love to go to conventions, retreats and fitness expos. In many ways what they do is an end in itself rather than a means to an end. They will block out whole weeks and cancel sessions or classes to prioritise a training course. They need a second household income as they never make any profit from what they do.

The 'busy but broke' business

This is the therapist or teacher who measures their success by how busy they are. They are often heard to say things like, 'I usually work fifteen hours a day' or 'I can't remember the last time I had a day off'. They say this with a level of pride. I have definitely been through the phase of 'busy but broke'. At one time I was teaching four nights a week, working six days a week and teaching over thirty hours of classes a week plus running the business. When I first opened my studio the overheads were huge and I was paying off a big investment. If I'd ever worked out my hourly rate I think I would have cried! Fortunately for me this was short term but for many it's not and they get stuck in that 'busy but broke' stage.

Which one of the above business types most resonates with you? Do you know of other people in your field operating their business in any of these ways? I hope you can see that these three ways of working are easy traps into which you can fall. It is very easy to think that because you are busy, or because you are really helping people, or because you can afford that next course, you are also successful. You may well survive with this type of business but it is unlikely you will thrive.

Keep this in mind as we look at the next common problem that small businesses face - working on your own.

CHAPTER THREE

Lone Worker Syndrome

▼

Yoga Teachers, Sports Massage Practitioners, Osteopaths, Pilates Teachers and many people with a Health and Fitness business are sole traders. As a sole trader, you are likely to spend some time, maybe even all your time, working on your own and using part of your home as your office.

When I first started teaching Pilates, I taught private clients at my house and also did all my business admin from a spare bedroom that I turned into an office.

Running your business from home sounds ideal. Doing your admin in your pyjamas with a big cup of tea, no commuting, spending more time with your family, may sound attractive. Working for yourself means you are your own boss, you work when you want to and will be answerable to no one.

Sadly, the reality can be somewhat different, as these six common problems illustrate:

Life/Work Balance

Life and, in particular, family life gets in the way. As your office is the kitchen table or an upstairs bedroom, work is always temptingly close. You can end up working longer hours and actually be more distracted and disconnected from your family. You find yourself thinking about work even when you're trying to spend time with your family, because your office is there in your home. It's just too tempting to deal with those emails at midnight, after the kids have gone to bed!

One Day

Procrastination. You sit down to get your accounts up to date and deal with some emails. Two hours later, you are still playing with Facebook, convincing yourself it is useful marketing time. Or you suddenly have an overwhelming urge to clean the fridge! With no one supervising you or checking in on your progress, it's very easy to get distracted.

Noticed

When you are a lone worker, you might struggle to be noticed. If you don't have premises or work out of a centre, then you won't get passing trade or as much cross referral. You may worry that this will impact on your credibility. If you see clients in your home, will your business be perceived as just a hobby?

Energy

How self-motivated are you? Even when you are passionate about what you do, it is hard to stay energised and motivated. You may discover that it was actually the team around you and the boss checking up on you that consistently drove you along when you were employed. We all like to think that we are self-starters and that if we worked for ourselves, we'd be driven and productive 24/7. The truth often falls a little way short of this as, left to our own devices, the energy may wane.

Limits

You may find that working from home places restrictions on the physical space you have to grow your business and get work done. Do you really have space at home for an office, that's not being used by someone else? I used to teach private Pilates clients from home before I opened Barefoot Studio. Home was a great place to start from as the overheads were very low. However, it was no good if someone in the room adjacent was watching TV or if the dog started barking her head off at a cat passing the window, or the neighbours' kids were running around screaming outside my window. Once they were even peering in. In the end, I had to limit the times of the day I could use my home studio for clients, which limited my income.

You

This is probably the big one... it's just you. You may have a supportive partner or great friends, but at the end of the day it's your business and it comes down to you. There's no IT team to fix the printer or colleague to help you write that tricky email. Often you can feel isolated and lacking support. Without colleagues, bosses, customers popping in, you realise that working at home can be silent and lonely. There's no Monday morning gossip over a cup of tea, no more birthday cake at team meetings. You may discover that working in a solitary environment is actually quite difficult for you. Long periods of working by yourself can lead to self-doubt. Experts suggest that working from home can isolate people from social networks and career opportunities whilst fostering a grazing instinct that keeps dangerous stress hormones at persistently high levels. If you are constantly picking at work your stress levels never get the chance to come down and this can ultimately affect quality of sleep.[1]

Working for yourself may lead you to feel burned out, de-motivated, lonely and a little lost but it can also be amazingly rewarding. The good news is that through following the five steps outlined in Part Two, you can build a Virtual Team around you and get the support you need. So, even if you work predominantly on your own, you always have people to whom you can turn.

---

1   Prof Gail Kinman, occupational health psychologist, University of Bedfordshire and the British Psychological Association.

Before you begin

Before you start planning your happy and profitable business, it is important to understand and reflect honestly on where you are today. Part One should have started you thinking about your own attitude to business and how you organise your working life.

Take a moment to ask yourself a few questions. Do you believe in your heart that you deserve to earn money from what you do or do you feel bad about charging people? Do you run your business more like a hobby, are you running around so busily that you really don't pause to work out if it what you do is profitable? Are you so focussed on what your clients need that you neglect your own needs? How have you found working for yourself? Do you recognise any of the symptoms of lone worker syndrome?

In Part Two I will offer some practical solutions to these problems. As you work through the five steps of the *Thrive* model and complete the **DO! EXERCISES**, you will start to build a clear framework and plan for your business.

For now though, let's take stock of where you are at present:

DO! EXERCISE

PAUSE AND REVIEW

▶ Ask yourself the following questions and make a note of them in your journal. If you are just starting out in business, then take stock of how you feel about these aspects of running a business right now. What aspects of running your own business do you think will come easily and what, if anything, are you dreading. If you are already up and running, then reflect on where you are to date:

- How do you feel about being in business?
- Which aspects of your business do you enjoy and which aspects do you not enjoy or avoid all together
- Without getting into the detail, what are your current income levels compared with what you had hoped for when you started
- Who is your main customer? Profile their age, gender, occupation.
- Roughly how many people do you currently work with?
- Are there any emerging new groups of people with whom you would like to work? For example, is there a health issue that is becoming more prominent in the media.
- What do you currently charge for your services? Do you feel you under charge, over charge or charge correctly?
- What are your operational costs? These are fixed costs like insurance, rent, professional membership etc.?
- What has your income, expenditure and profit and loss been like to date?
- Were there any unforeseen expenditures in the last twelve months?
- Are you anticipating any additional one off expenditure in the next twelve months, for example buying new equipment, re-developing your website?
- Do you have a marketing strategy?
- What works well for you in marketing and what does not?

* Where do most of your clients come from? What are your top three sources of new clients?

* How do you communicate what you do?

* What aspects of running your business challenged you in the last twelve months?

* What lessons have your learnt, if any, from any mistakes that have happened this year?

* How is your work/life balance?

* Is any aspect of managing the business overwhelming you?

* When did you last have a holiday?
  How many days off did you have in the last twelve months? Do you have at least one full business free day a week?

* Do you need to build in more down time?

* Have you had access to the support you've needed in the last twleve months?

* What single thing would make running your business easier or more enjoyable?

How to Thrive

'My mission in life is not merely to survive, but to thrive; and to do so with some passion, some compassion, some humour, and some style'

Maya Angelou

American Poet and Civil Rights Activist

The Secret to a Happy and Profitable Business

Over the last sixteen years I have trained hundreds of Pilates and Nordic Walking Instructors and worked with many therapists. Far too many of these people, despite being talented at what they do, barely survive in business. It saddens me when some people ultimately decide to stop practising when the only thing they needed was a bit of business guidance.

Part Two of this book is all about giving you that guidance. It offers a clear set of steps to give you the best chance of succeeding in business and also enjoying the process.

From talking to many people and by tapping into my own experience of setting up and running Barefoot Studio, I have come up with a five step method to help you find the secret to a happy and profitable Health and Fitness business. It is simple, easy to implement and it works. Just work your way through the 5 Ms:

- **Mindset** – think like a business person and value what you do
- **Map** – know where you want to be and identify your ideal customer
- **Monetise** – calculate how much to charge and explore new ideas for developing income streams
- **Market** – attract paying customers who value what you do
- **Manage** – learn to streamline admin tasks and be time-efficient

Hopefully you completed the **DO! EXERCISE** at the end of Part One. This will give you a clear benchmark against which to measure your progress. Keep a record of this in your journal to refer to later.

CHAPTER FOUR

MINDSET

STEP
1

Mindset – Get a Business Head On

The first step towards developing any great business is to start thinking like a business person. I'm going to look at your mindset and help you to 'Get a business head on'. This involves understanding that being an authentic, value-based business is an asset and is not at odds with making a profit. I'm going to ask you to drill down into the true value of what you do for your client and to think less in terms of money for your time and more in terms of being paid for the solutions you offer. We will also look at some of the key elements of running a successful business and the tools available to help.

Primarily, I want you to understand that you actually are in business and that you have invested a huge amount of time and money to get where you are today, i.e. a qualified and talented therapist or teacher. More training alone is never the answer _ you have to get your business head on!

Here are some statements people have often made to me about what they do:

'*It is not a business.*'
Professional Counsellor with no other source of income

'*I feel bad charging people as they need my help so much.*'
Nutritional Therapist who had studied for three years

'*Who would want to pay that kind of money to spend an hour with me?*'
Newly-qualified Pilates Teacher

So many therapists and teachers don't view what they do as a business. The definition of a business as found in the Oxford English Dictionary is:

'*A person's regular occupation, profession, or trade or a commercial activity*'

If you would like to earn a living, full or part time, from being a therapist or a fitness instructor, then you are going to be running a business. This means knowing what your costs are, charging appropriately so that you make a profit, setting goals for the number of clients you need in order to make a good income and regularly reviewing how you are performing. It doesn't mean you have to write lengthy business plans or be driven purely by profit.

You can offer an authentic service and also run a real business

Some of the really great businesses out there are not actually driven by money but have a far more ethical primary purpose. However, the profit ensures that the business can continue to provide that purpose.

It would be very easy to assume that business people and entrepreneurs are motivated purely by money and making as much of it as possible. The truth is somewhat different. Look at just three big business success stories and you'll see a very different motivation.

Dame Anita Roddick founded The Bodyshop in 1976. Yes, she wanted to create a livelihood for herself and her family but she also had a very clear vision. The Body Shop uses its stores and products to help communicate human rights and environmental issues. The more profitable they became the more positive is the impact they can have on human rights and the environment. Early in 2016 The Body Shop reaffirmed this commitment by stating its aim to become the world's most ethical and sustainable global business. The brand believes its new focus will help it to become: 'Both a force for good and a successful, profitable business'.

Steve Jobs, co-founder of Apple, was quoted on many occasions as saying that being rich, or making money was not what motivated him in business, he said, 'Going to bed at night saying we've done something wonderful, that's what matters to me'. Steve Jobs' vision was to get a computer into the hands of everyday people. Designed for beginners, the user-friendly Apple II was a tremendous success, ushering in the era of the personal computer.

Richard Branson famously said, 'I have never gone into any business purely to make money. If money is your only motive, then I believe you shouldn't launch that business at all'. Richard Branson fundamentally believes that doing good is good for business, and that we should all work in a way that puts the focus on caring for people, communities and the planet.

Today, increasing value is placed on businesses that are seen as authentic. Being true to who you are, what you do and whom you serve makes your business stand out in a crowded market place. When you buy a product or service from an authentic business, it feels good. Pick up a bargain from a money driven business and it just feels cheap.

Most people working in the Health and Fitness sector want to improve people's lives and this is a good thing! Just remember that it's okay to make a good living wage helping others.

Valuing what you do – are you allergic to money?

Despite being talented at what we do, achieving great results and being motivated by an altruistic goal, we don't always associate all this with a monetary value or even value ourselves. Beware that little voice in your head that says, 'But it's only me, doing my thing, I can't really expect people to pay for this'.

We can actually talk ourselves into a mindset of not deserving an income. Do you think you do this? Are you allergic to money? I want you to change your thinking on what you really do for your clients. Stop thinking about it in terms of time or an hourly rate and start thinking about the problems you solve, the way you make them feel in body, mind and spirit.

How would you value someone's service if they could:

- Take someone who is in pain, teach them to enjoy moving again, pain free, so they can get back to gardening which they love?

- Take someone who is plagued with depression and anxiety and teach them to feel safe and confident enough to travel to their daughter's graduation?

- Take someone who has struggled with their weight their whole life and teach them to stop linking emotions with food and to be free from constant dieting?

- Take a lifelong runner who has had to give up running through injury, and get them to the point where they complete a 10K race?

Can you see that what is on offer is so much more than an hour of your time, or just a workout, or therapy session. Remember you are not just selling yourself!

In the next **DO! EXERCISE**, I want you to think about the services you offer and the value of this to your clients. Have an actual person in mind when you do this.

For example, I have a Pilates one-to-one client called Janice. She has a stressful life as a carer for her elderly mum, she works part time and has a long-term back problem that will keep recurring if she doesn't exercise regularly and keep moving. She spends all week thinking about other people and putting herself last.

Service you offer	What they get	What they really get, i.e. what are all the benefits?
Pilates one-to-one	60-minute session 1x a week	Pain free for 95% of the time An hour (away from her life) in a peaceful environment The chance to chat to me about her week I give her exercises to work on at home She fully relaxes in the session as she has to concentrate. She then goes home feeling refreshed
	VALUE £	VALUE £

What value do you think Janice places on that one hour session of Pilates? Do you think she calculates the value based on time or on the actual service? Put yourself in her shoes and value it from what it means to her and her life.

Complete the following **DO! EXERCISE** using examples from people you have worked with and helped. We will come back to this in a later chapter.

DO! EXERCISE

Fill in this table:

Service you offer	What they get	What they really get, i.e. what are all the benefits?

The 'training drain' – why getting more qualifications won't get you more customers

It is a commonly held myth that the more qualifications you have, the more customers you will attract. Yes, we all need to be qualified in the area of Health and Fitness on which our business is based. However, your level of qualification is unlikely to be your best marketing tool (we will look at marketing in detail in a later chapter). Spending time and money on yet another course or qualification bolsters our confidence and may help to quieten that inner voice that constantly tells us we are a fraud, but does it really drive more customers to our business?

Ask yourself, when did you last ask a hairdresser how many years it took them to qualify and what their colouring qualification actually is? Have you ever asked your Doctor or

Dentist where they trained and or when did they last go on a professional development course (CPD)?

Now ask yourself what percentage of your clients have ever asked you what your qualifications are and how many of them actually know what your qualifications mean. For example, I am a certified REPs (Register of Exercise Professionals) Level 4 Pilates teacher. Most of my clients have never heard of REPs, wouldn't know what it stands for and, unless they have read the 'about me' section of my website, probably don't even know I have this qualification.

Business principles – getting your head around running a business

Running a business is very simple once you stop being an ostrich and look at what needs to be done.

There are five key admin and management tasks you need to keep on top of and there are some fabulous tools out there to help you with this and to keep this admin and management to a minimum:

1. **Planning:** The second step of the 5 Ms of *Thrive* is all about knowing where you are going so you can then plan how to get there. It is essential that you actually take time to think about how many clients you specifically need, when you want to work, how long you are going to give yourself to build up your business etc. We are going to explore this in detail in the next section, MAP.

2. **Money in – Money out:** We will explore this in detail in Step 3 which deals with how to monetise your business. You should have a good idea whether or not you are on track to hit your targets for the level of income you need. This means a minimum of a quick review of income and expen-

diture at least monthly. For any session, class, course or workshop that you run, you must know what the break-even number of bookings are based on your rate card. Quite simply you must keep a record of all the income and expenditure that passes through your business.

3. **Rate card and cancellation policies:** Again, we will explore this in some detail in Step 3. You need to work out what you are going to charge for all of the services that you offer and if you are going to discount for packaged services or buying a number of sessions up front. This menu of prices and services is what I will refer to as your 'rate card'. Even if it is a few pence you must increase your charges annually. Then you need to decide on a cancellation policy and stick to it 100% of the time.

4. **Client records and bookings:** You need to capture data of all the people who pass through your business, from initial enquiries to actual clients. Most people with Health and Fitness businesses also collect personal and health information about their clients. You need to make sure this information is kept confidential and also securely. You will want to track appointments and bookings for classes or sessions. There are some great on-line tools on the market for this which we will explore in Step 5 MANAGE.

5. **Communication:** How are customers going to get hold of you and when or how much time are you going to allocate to this. I have a golden rule for communication that I stick to rigidly:

Only respond to emails, phone calls and social media messages during office hours

For me this means Monday to Friday 9am to 6pm and Saturday mornings between 9am and 12noon.

This approach has two massive benefits:

1. It gives a clear message that you are a professional business, operating in business hours and that you are not available 24/7. Be clear with your customers and they will know what to expect.

2. It enables you to switch off from work! If you allow yourself to respond to emails at midnight just before you go to bed or to keep checking emails on Sundays, then you will never switch off. This is a sure fire route to burnout.

I will talk more about setting your 'opening hours' in the final part of this book when I discuss how to sustain a happy business.

Summary

In this chapter, we have looked at the way you perceive the work that you do. I hope you have begun to understand that you are in business. You can be a real and profitable business and still be strongly based on values. What you actually deliver for your customers is of vital importance to them and can be valued in much greater terms than money for time. Just getting more and more qualifications, despite bolstering your confidence, won't get you more customers. In the last part of this chapter I outline some of the key day-to-day tasks involved in running a business professionally. You should now have your 'business head' on and be ready for the next steps!

The next **DO! EXERCISE** focuses on what you've invested to date in your business in terms of both time and money. Quite simply, when you understand the cost of your 'goods' you will have a better idea of the value of your 'product' and therefore how to charge. It wasn't until I did this exercises myself that I fully understood how much of an investment in both time and money I had made to become a Pilates teacher.

DO! EXERCISE

▶ **CALCULATE YOUR INVESTMENT TO DATE**

Open up a spreadsheet or just use a piece of paper.

Aim to total up the costs of:

- All of your professional training to date, including your initial qualification, CPD (continuing professional development), further courses etc.

- Travel and expenses to attend courses.

- Books and materials you have bought to support your study.

- Equipment and clothing you needed to start up.

- How long has it taken you to gain your qualification?

- Any printed materials or marketing materials (e.g. website) that you used to launch your business.

Keep a note of the total figure in your journal. You will need to refer back to this in Step 3 MONETISE.

At the end of Part One you reflected on where you are on your journey to building a happy and profitable Health and Fitness business. In the last **DO! EXERCISE** you calculated your investment in time and money. Now let's start to look at where you want to go.

CHAPTER FIVE

Map

'If you don't know where
you're going, you're liable to
end up someplace else'

Lawrence Peter 'Yogi' Berra
(Baseball Player and Manager)

Step 2 of the 5 Ms method is to clearly map out what you want and to imagine what it will feel like to be there. At this point I want you to let go of any thinking that will limit you. Set your road map with a head that believes and a heart that is looking forward to the journey.

You are going to map out where you want to be in three ways. First, to set clear targets for you in terms of where you want to work, when, how often and for how much income. Second, you need to identify your tribe, who they are, where they hang out and what they need. Third, and importantly, you are going to put all this within the context of a time frame. At the end, you are going to stress test your plan to check that all three elements work together to move you forward with ease.

Target: map out your lifestyle business

When you are planning your business you have the opportunity to design a way of working that is unique and specific to you, your dreams and your aspirations. In reality we all have to work outside of this ideal at times, but start with mapping out the ideal and then decide where the compromises or stepping stones are.

Most people in the Health and Fitness sector have to work some anti-social hours but you need to be realistic about how much of this you can do. When I first opened Barefoot Studio I was teaching four nights a week. In the short term I had to do this to pay the bills but it was not sustainable. I now teach two nights a week and on the days I work late, I don't come into work until midday.

For the purposes of the following **DO! EXERCISE,** I want you to plan your ideal. Don't limit yourself, imagine the perfect work/life balance. What would this look like?

DO! EXERCISE

► *As best you can answer the following questions:*

WHERE?

* How far from your home do you want to travel to deliver sessions or classes?

* Do you want to work from home or from other premises. This could be hiring a village hall to run classes or renting a treatment room?

* Do you want to be part of an existing wellness centre, studio, gym?

* Do you need other people around when you are working, e.g. for safety?

WHEN?

* How many hours a week do you want to work in face-to-face service delivery?

- How many sessions or classes can you deliver in a block and still maintain quality?
- How many days a week do you want to work?
- What time of day do you want to work? Mornings, afternoons, evenings?
- If you said you are happy to work evenings, how many evenings would you be willing to work in a week?
- Are you happy to work weekends?
- Do you need to take the school holidays off?
- Are there any times in the day when you absolutely cannot work, e.g., during the school run?

▶ *Draw out a timetable for a typical working week and add up the face-to-face customer hours you would be working. Next take a moment to write down how much money you would like to earn:*

- To what level of income do you aspire?
- What is the minimum income you need?

These two bits of mapped out information will be essential when you start to look at Step 3 MONETISE. They will help you do some simple calculations to work out what you need to be charging to reach your desired income levels.

For now, let's go on to map out with whom you are going to be working.

Identifying your Tribe – who, where, when and what they need

A common mistake that many new Therapists and Fitness Teachers make is to fail to identify and get to know their Tribe.

Know that 80% of your clients will fit into the demographic of your target market or Tribe. This doesn't mean you will turn away the other 20%, but it will help you to hone your marketing. Crucially your Tribe must be compatible with your own personal targets. It may seem obvious, but it's no good wanting to work with professional 25-35 year olds if you only want to work weekday mornings.

Knowing your Tribe will help you to pinpoint your marketing with real precision and enable you to hone your service to exactly meet the needs of your Tribe. In many ways your specific Tribe is the very paper on which your business map is printed. Once you know your Tribe and know everything about your Tribe, the rest of your map will flow from it in a logical sequence:

- Know your Tribe
- Understand your Tribe's pain or problem
- Know your Tribe's hopes
- Provide a solution specific to your Tribe

For now, we are going to focus on the first item, 'knowing your Tribe'.

If your Health and Fitness business is already up and running, then reflect on which demographic makes up the lion's share of your client base. If you are just starting out, then think about the particular group of people who you feel you can help. Maybe you identify with them yourself, or perhaps they are available at the same times you want to work.

DO! EXERCISE

IDENTIFY YOUR TRIBE

▶ Remember as you do this exercise you are seeking to identify the core of your market, this is the group of people with whom you will be predominantly working. It is a niche and you need a niche. Don't be afraid to be too narrow at this point:

DEMOGRAPHIC

- How old are they?
- Are they men or women, or both?
- Where do they hang out?
- What do they like to read?
- When is their free time?
- What level is their disposable income?
- What do they do for a living?
- What hobbies or interests do they have?

DISTANCE

▶ Make a list of the top three geographical areas your tribe live in:

1. Number one might be your home town
2. and 3 will then be within a distance you are willing to travel regularly, or are such hotspots for your tribe that it's worth locating your business there and commuting. If, you can offer your service over the internet using something like Skype then number 3 could be anywhere!

▶ Start thinking about yourself as a specialist. Imagine you are at a party and someone asks you what you do. In the following examples, A is a person who is very generalist and B is a person who knows their tribe:

> A: 'I'm a Counsellor'
> B: 'I'm a Counsellor and I specialise in women with ante-natal depression'

> A: 'I'm a Pilates Teacher'
> B: 'I'm a Pilates Teacher and I specialise in people with long-term chronic back pain'

> A: 'I'm a Nutritional Therapist'
> B: 'I'm a Nutritional Therapist and I work with teenagers'

> A: 'I'm a Yoga Teacher'
> B: I'm a Yoga Teacher and I work with the over fifty-fives to keep them flexible'

In Step 4 MARKET, we will really get to know your Tribe. You are going to immerse yourself in their world and learn to understand the specific problem or need that you and your business can potentially address.

Next you need to decide how long it is going to take you to reach your lifestyle business targets of where and when you want to work and how much you want to earn.

Timescales

It's important when mapping out where you want to go, to have an idea about how long the journey is going to take.

If you have been following through the mapping process, then you will have written down how much your ideal income needs to be and how many hours a week you want to work. The next step is to set a clear deadline for when your business has built up enough to reach these targets.

If you are just starting out, then you may not yet be generating any income from your Health and Fitness business. If you have been operating for a while you will know your income currently. Either way, use this as your baseline.

DO! EXERCISE

▶ Ask yourself at what point in the future would you like or need to be earning the income you identified? Will it take six months, twelve months?

▶ Set a time-specific goal and record it: By x date I will be generating x amount of income from my Health and Fitness business.

In the next step, MONETISE, you will be able to use this business map and your income targets to help you structure the services you offer and to set your rate card. You will then be able to see how quickly you need to grow your business in order to reach your target within your timescale.

Lifestyle vs Tribe vs Income – stress test your model

The final step of mapping your business is to do a simple stress test. Do the three elements of target, tribe and timescale match up?

Here is an example case study:

Jane is a newly qualified Pilates Instructor. She has two children of school age and is restarting work having taken a career break to have a family. Jane wants to fit her teaching around her family commitments as much as possible.

Target

Jane wants to work a maximum of fifteen hours a week in face-to-face teaching hours. Five hours of this will be group classes and ten hours will be private one-to-one sessions. Jane does not want to work weekends but is happy to work one night a week. She wants to work in the town in which she lives and does not want to have to travel more than thirty minutes to a teaching venue. Jane has a space in her house where she can offer one-to-one private sessions and she is researching the hire of village halls for group classes. Jane's group classes wouldn't run in the school holidays but she would still teach her private one-to-one classes when possible. Jane would like to earn approx. £20,000 a year.

Tribe

Jane wants to work with mums looking to exercise in the daytime. This will form 80% of her client base and is her niche.

How old are they?	25-45
Are they men or women, or both?	Women
Where do they hang out?	After school drop off many of the mums meet for coffee in one of the town's cafés. There is an active Tennis Club and Book Group.
What do they like to read?	There is a free local newspaper that is read by many. The town has a Facebook hub page that is well visited.
When is their free time?	Mornings are the best times, especially immediately after the school run.
What level is their disposable income?	The area is affluent with family incomes above £40,000. Other small group classes, like yoga, are around £10 per one hour lesson. Local PT instructors charge between £40 and £60 per session.
What do they do for a living?	Full time mum, some have part-time work.
What hobbies or interests do they have?	Tennis.
What brands or products do they use?	Generally interested in health for themselves and their families. Food shop at Waitrose. Natural skin care. Sweaty Betty clothing.

Timescale

Jane would like to reach her income goal within six months.

In this example, Jane is a member of the Tribe she wants to target. Therefore, her desired business lifestyle model fits with her Tribe. Her clients want to exercise at the same times Jane wants to work. Her income expectations are realistic and match with the number of hours she is willing to work. In reality, if her classes are a success, she could earn significantly more than the £20,000 to which she aspires.

DO! EXERCISE

STRESS TEST YOUR MODEL

► Go back over your notes on Target, Tribe and Timescale to check that they are compatible with each other. Ask yourself:

Is your Tribe available and wanting to work when you do?

Can your Tribe afford to pay the rate needed to reach your income target?

Is the size of your Tribe big enough to support your income level and timescale target or will you have to develop a second or third geographical market?

Summary

At the end of Step 2 MAP, you should have a clear idea of where you want to be by a specific future date. You should know exactly what your working week will look like and who your typical client is. You should have a clear expectation of when this will all be achievable.

There is a powerful energy in setting a clear intention. People, and more importantly your customers, will pick up on this energy. They will see that you are clear about what you offer, to whom and that you know where you want to be. A clear map makes it much easier to make decisions and to ensure that you don't waste energy and time. For example, you may be weighing up a training course that someone recommends to you. All you need do is ask yourself, 'Would taking this course move me along my journey to where I want to be?'.

Having a mapped-out business is like having a clear vision for the future. I know exactly what I want my business and lifestyle to be like next year, in three years' time and when I'm fifty-five. When someone offers me work, I stress test it with these three questions:

1. Will doing this help get me to where I want to be?

2. Do I absolutely love doing the thing that I'm being asked to do?

3. Does it pay so well that it's worth doing even if the answers to Questions 1 and 2 are 'no'?

The answer has to be yes to at least one of these questions and preferably to at least two of them. If the answer is yes to all three, then I know that the work I'm being offered aligns with my business map and is therefore right for me at that time.

Take the time to map out your perfect business and lifestyle so you know exactly where you want to be and how to get there.

In the next step, MONETISE, you will need to reach for your calculator as we are going to put some hard numbers against this map to ensure that your business is profitable.

CHAPTER SIX

STEP
3

MONETISE

Monetise

▼

The single biggest mistake that people make when they set up a Health and Fitness business is to undercharge.

In this step of the 5 Ms, MONETISE, you are going to ensure that your business pays, that you earn what you are genuinely worth, and that you value what you do.

By the end of this chapter you will have a clear pricing structure for what you do, with a cancellation policy to underpin it. You will have ideas for a range of revenue streams and a good understanding of your operational costs. We are also going to touch on managing your money so that it doesn't become an overwhelming task at the end of the Financial Year. Finally, I will ask you to work out how long it will take you to pay back the initial investment you made in your training and business.

I just want to make a comment on some of the terminology I'm going to be using in this section. I refer to the service you provide as 'products'. A product doesn't have to be a physical thing it can also be a service. So, for example, you might currently offer:

* one hour counselling session for one person
* one hour group exercise class
* one hour one-to-one personal training session
* thirty-minute sports massage treatment
* ninety-minute initial consultation

Think of each of these as an individual product.

'Cost of goods' is a term I use to reflect the cost of delivering each of your products, which will vary depending on how busy you are. 'Operational Costs' are the annual running costs, or to put it another way, the fixed costs of being in business.

Let's begin by putting this chapter into context. I'm sitting in a coffee shop writing this chapter on my laptop. I've just bought a cup of tea that cost me £2.50. Now, I could have made this cup of tea at home for the cost of one tea bag and a splash of milk _ probably for less than five pence. It took the woman behind the counter only five minutes to serve me but her time is a small part of the cost of that cup of tea. So, what am I really paying for? There are three members of staff behind the counter, the café is warm and nicely lit. I'm sitting on a comfy chair with a clean table in front of me. This café is paying rent and rates in a prime retail area. The cafe is playing background music for which they will have paid a music licence. The venue will be insured and all the staff need training. They probably have another three members of the staff team, one of whom may be on paid holiday, and they all get sick pay if needed. I could go on listing the true costs of that one cup of tea. The reality being that they probably didn't make a lot of money from selling it to me... they needed me to also buy a cake to make any profit from my visit!

I hope you can see how your time is just one small part of what you do. So move your thinking away from an hourly rate and drill down deep into your actual running costs. Factor in the true value of the service that you provide and then you will be getting close to what you should be charging for what you do.

Me vs product

As I mentioned, the single biggest mistake that people make when they set up a Health and Fitness business is to undercharge.

Undercharging comes from a simple mistake in the way we think as therapists and fitness instructors. We start from the premise that we are selling ourselves and that we are the product. This way of thinking is fundamentally flawed for three reasons:

1. You are actually in the business of solving your customers' problems. For your client, the outcome of the session or treatment they have will usually have a much higher value than if you value it purely on money for time.

2. Most of us will undervalue ourselves because of lack of confidence or self-worth. That little voice in your head that says, 'It's only me, who would pay x to spend an hour with me'.

3. If you only factor your time into the equation you will miss many of the costs hidden behind that one hour of your time and you are likely to get your pricing wrong.

It is essential that you value what you do and don't under-charge. Hopefully the earlier **DO! EXERCISE** will have made you think about charging for your product rather than charging for you.

I want you to change your thinking on what you actually do for your clients. Stop thinking about it in terms of time or an hourly rate and start thinking about the problems you solve; the unique solution you provide to your Tribe's 'pain'; the way you make your clients feel in body mind and spirit.

Owning the value of what you offer the world creates a power-ful ripple effect around you. You offer better work, earn more, have more resources to take care of the people and things you care about and become an example of what is possible for the people you set out to help.

I want you to keep this mindset while you work through the entire MONETISE step.

Exploring multiple revenue streams

If you are a therapist, you are likely to work primarily on a one-to-one basis delivering a treatment to a single person at a time. As a fitness instructor, you may also work on a one-to-one basis, for example as a personal trainer. A fitness instructor is also likely to run group classes, typically an hour in length. For example, a Yoga or Pilates group class. For many of you, this will be your core business.

However, I would like you to think about other possible income streams. Consider:

- ◆ Extended classes or workshops
- ◆ Day courses
- ◆ Holidays and weekend retreats

* Speaking at an event
* Corporate in-house workshops
* On-line courses
* A downloadable article or class
* A retail product

Let's look at these in a bit more detail:

Extended classes or workshops

At Barefoot Studio, we offer a range of two hour workshops that we put on as stand-alone one off events. The following are examples of two hour workshops that we have offered:

* Introduction to Nordic Walking
* Pilates for neck pain
* Mobilising the spine
* Everyday posture – taking Pilates into your everyday life
* Taking Pilates to the next level
* Therapist taster session
* Pilates equipment taster session
* Seasonal specific course or class, e.g., ski fit or get in shape for summer

Other ideas might be a workshop on healthy eating, mindfulness or massage skills for the family or stretching for runners.

Workshops are a way of attracting new customers. They can be used to create a marketing buzz around the promotion of a specific event. They are also an add on product for existing customers.

Day courses

You may have enough material to offer full day courses. This could be done by yourself or in partnership with another therapist or fitness instructor.

At Barefoot Studio, we have run a number of one day courses. On one occasion, we partnered with a nutritional therapist and a mindfulness teacher to run a one-day course on weight management. I delivered the exercise part, the nutritional therapist talked about food and the mindfulness coach ran a section on our emotional relationship with food. These types of events are great for cross-referral and attracting new clients.

Holidays and weekend retreats

There is a growing trend towards anti-ageing, fitness and wellness holidays. In part this has been fuelled by the ageing baby boomers wanting to stay youthful and enjoy an active lifestyle. This demographic also has disposable income and is willing to spend it on experiences that enhance their lives.

You don't have to be offering a two-week Yoga Retreat in Thailand! You can start small, partnering with a local hotel or B&B to put on a short break. You could arrange a retreat weekend for you and your clients, where you make the arrangements and deliver the element of the weekend that is orientated around the therapy or fitness activity.

Wellness holidays are particularly popular among 30+ men and women who lead busy lives and are themselves success-ful business people. If you are not taking your own clients on this kind of trip, you may need to identify a specific tribe to target and hone your marketing accordingly.

Speaking at an event

There are many opportunities to share your passion for what you do by speaking at everything from Health Fairs and Conferences to WI meetings. It is true that you won't always get a Speaker's Fee at these events, but they are undoubtedly fantastic marketing opportunities.

It is well worth always having a number of short, twenty- to thirty-minute, presentations ready to go. If possible, the presentations should include PowerPoint slides with lots of images, an actual experience of what you do, your personal story and testimonials. It's important to end with a 'call to action', maybe sign up for a six-week course today and get one extra session free, for example.

Prepare a one sheet summary of the type of talks you can offer with all your contact details and a short biog. If you have them, include testimonials from other Event Organisers who can recommend you as a speaker. You can then use this document to send out to prospective events, at which you could speak.

Corporate in-house workshops/team building

More and more companies are becoming switched on to the fact that healthy employees are key to their business. The benefits are numerous: less sick leave, improved productivity, improved morale and staff retention, plus less stress. It is often simple to re-package what you do to target this specific market.

Here are just some examples:

Yoga/Pilates teacher or Personal Trainer:
Stretching at your desk

Osteopath or Pilates teacher: Back health in
the workplace

Nutritional Therapist: Healthy eating on the go

Counsellor, Yoga Teacher: Reducing stress at work

Nordic Walking Instructor: Business net-walking

You could also just come up with a workshop that is fun, gets the team interacting and moving as a team building type experience.

The joy of a corporate product is that the organisation will provide the venue and the attendees. You would usually agree a fixed fee and, in effect, just show up.

Online courses

This may not be applicable to all types of Health and Fitness businesses but internet based services are an increasingly popular way of working. If you are able to work with people via webinars or offer one-to-one coaching using Skype, for example, then you open out to a potentially global market.

Counselling, nutrition coaching and mindfulness training, are all therapies that can successfully be delivered in this way. I have even taught one-to-one Pilates using Skype.

Not all online products need be live. Think about whether you can develop any products that could be bought and downloaded, like an article, class or podcast. With modern gadgets, it is relatively simple to make good quality video/ sound recordings or digital images which can be shared.

The benefit of offering your services online is that there are no premises or travel costs for you. It also helps to raise your business profile.

A retail product

Not all Health and Fitness businesses are suited to traditional retail products. However, for some there are relevant products that could be sold as an additional income stream. For example, some massage therapists sell aromatherapy oils and creams. If you are a Pilates or Yoga Instructor you could sell props, mats and other small equipment or products like Toesox. Nordic Walking Instructors may have the opportunity to sell poles. It is also worth exploring forming a partnership with a local shop. For a therapist, this could be a Health Food shop or for someone in the fitness industry it could be a Sports Retailer. If the shop is an independent retailer you might be able to negotiate commission for referring your clients to them or at the very least have a reciprocal marketing arrangement.

The above list of suggestions is not exhaustive. Ultimately the ideal is to find products which you can sell that do not require you to be there to deliver them. This way you can still be earning an income even when you are taking some well-earned holiday time. There are some amazing and affordable on-line platforms available that make e-commerce very accessible. Shopify provides a professional retail platform with fees that are based on what you sell rather than a fixed monthly amount. More simply you can just have a few products that you sell in person when you are face-to-face with clients.

DO! EXERCISE

▶ Write out a list, of the 'products' you are going to offer as part of your business. Specify:

- ◆ Name of product
- ◆ Frequency – for example, weekly, monthly, one off
- ◆ Number of units available

For example:

NAME: Pilates Beginners group class

FREQUENCY: Weekly

NUMBER OF UNITS
  AVAILABLE: 12 people per class = 12 units

NAME: Introduction to Nordic Walking workshop

FREQUENCY: Monthly

NUMBER OF UNITS
  AVAILABLE: 15 people per workshop = 15 units

Hopefully you now have an exciting menu of 'products' that you can offer. Before you work out what to charge for each of these products, you need to calculate your operational or running costs.

Knowing your operational costs

Before you can decide what to charge, you have to know exactly what it costs you to run your business and the true cost of each and every product you deliver. Operational costs fall into two main categories:

1. Operational or fixed costs that you incur regardless of how busy you are or how many products you sell. For example, insurance and professional membership. In other words, regardless of whether or not you had a customer you would still need to pay these costs.

2. Variable costs that relate directly to an individual product. These are sometimes called the cost of goods. The total cost of these will increase the more products you sell. For example, it may cost you £12 an hour to hire a treatment room, 50p per treatment for oils and couch roll and £1 per hour to park outside the therapy rooms you hire. So, the cost of delivering a one-hour massage is £13.50. In other words, if you don't get a booking you don't pay this cost.

NOTE: It is important to know what the latest time is that you can cancel a service before incurring any of the cost of goods. This will help inform your cancellation policy. So for example, if the owner of the treatment room you hire still charges you full rent if you cancel the room with less than twenty-four hours' notice, then your cancellation policy needs to be at least twenty-four hours.

The following exercise will enable you to work out your annual running or operational costs:

DO! EXERCISE

▶ Complete the following chart to calculate your total fixed operational costs per year. Add in any other categories of expenditure that you pay regardless of the number of clients you have.

OPERATIONAL COSTS CHECK LIST	£
Insurance	1200
Printing and stationery	1000
Marketing	2000
Website	1000
Professional membership	1200
Subscriptions to professional listings	1000
Continuing professional development	1000
Equipment wear and tear	1000
Phone and postage	
Internet	1500
Accountancy fees	2000
Music licence	600
	12,500

Now go on to calculate the 'cost of goods' for a typical service that you deliver. Again, add in costs that are relevant to the services that you provide.

COST OF GOODS	£
Room hire	———
Travel and expenses	———
Consumables, e.g. massage oils	———
Laundry, e.g. clean towels for every client	———

Setting your rate card

Your rate card is like a menu in a restaurant, it sets out all the products you sell and the price to the customer. When deciding what to charge for your service or product you need to consider two factors:

1. The actual and full costs of delivering that service or product

2. The genuine value of the outcome of that service or product to your customer.

Firstly, it is really important that you know exactly how every service you offer stacks up financially.

If you offer a service that you sell to more than one person, for example, a group exercise class, you must know how many people need to attend for you to break even. If the service you offer is only ever delivered to one person, you need to know the minimum charge to cover those costs.

All the information you have captured so far will help you make this simple calculation:

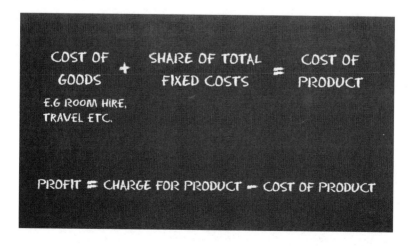

Let's go back to our example of Jane, who is setting up in business as a Pilates teacher.

Jane's annual fixed operational costs are:

	£
Insurance	£100
Printing and stationery	£50
Marketing	£100
Website	£150
Professional membership	£200
Subscriptions to professional listings	£75
Continuing professional development	£450
Equipment wear and tear	£100
Phone and postage	£200
Accountancy fees	£100
Music licence	£100
Class booking software	£450
TOTAL	**£2,075**

As part of mapping out her business, Jane identified that she wants to work 15 hours per week. Based on working 42 weeks of the year this equates to 630 hours of face-to-face service provision. Therefore, the per session cost of Jane's operational costs is £2,075 divided by 630, which equals £3.30. This needs to be added to the cost of the individual product or service:

Jane offers two main products, group Pilates (maximum twelve people per class) and one-to-one private sessions.

Group Class	£
Hire of village hall	£20
Travel	Nil
Share of fixed costs	£3.30
Total cost of product	£23.30

Example A. If Jane only charged £5 per person for the class she would need five people to break even. If she had ten people attending the class she would make £26.70 for the class.

Example B. If Jane charged £10 for the class per person she would need three people to break even. If she had ten people attending the class she would make £66.70 for the class.

What Jane also needs to factor in is how much time does it take her to prepare for the class and if there is any travel time. Let's assume it took her thirty minutes to plan her class, fifteen minutes to travel there and fifteen minutes to travel back. In model A this would make her hourly rate £13.35 an hour with ten people attending and in Model B £33.35 an hour with ten people attending.

Working out the cold, hard profit and loss of every product you offer is one way to set your rate card and is an important place to start. However, this is only the first step. You then need to calculate the value of the solution you provide to your customer and add this in to your pricing.

DO! EXERCISE

▶ Choose two of your most frequently delivered services and calculate the true cost of delivering this product, using the following formula:

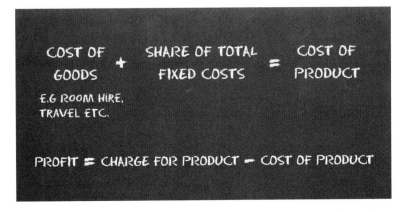

COST OF GOODS + SHARE OF TOTAL FIXED COSTS = COST OF PRODUCT

E.G ROOM HIRE, TRAVEL ETC.

PROFIT = CHARGE FOR PRODUCT − COST OF PRODUCT

Once you have worked out the cost of delivering each product, add on the profit margin based on the real value to the customer. This will give you your retail price for that product. Reflect back on the **DO! EXERCISE** you completed in Step 1 MINDSET, where you listed the value of what your product delivers for your customer. What are the real outcomes for your client, for example, able to run again, no more back pain, less anxiety? What do you think they would be willing to pay for that kind of result?

The charge for each product you offer should give a worthwhile profit margin for you and also reflect the value of what you offer to your customer.

Repeat this exercise for every type of session or class that you offer. Revisit your table of products and add your pricing against each item.

Remember it is always easier to offer a discount or to lower your prices than it is to increase them.

In the next section, I'll give you some examples of how you can offer great value to your regular clients without undervaluing what you do.

Block bookings, passes and discounts

Once you have calculated your rate card for every service you offer, you can then look at packaging up sessions to incentivise bulk buying. Bulk buying should always be a win/win for you and your client. You get a chunk of money in advance and the security of knowing that a series of sessions are pre-booked and pre-sold. They get a good price for committing up front and paying in advance for a number of sessions.

The simplest model for discounting in this way is: **The more sessions you buy, the cheaper it gets**. The following example shows how this would work for a Pilates Matwork group class, where the maximum class size is twelve people:

Single class	£12 (pay as you go)
Block of six classes	£66, i.e. £11 a class
Block of twelve classes	£120, i.e. £10 a class

The product you will sell the most of is the middle one. You need to ensure that if all twelve people in your class paid for their classes at this level, you make the income you need to make it profitable. The single class price should be at a high enough price that it actually puts people off buying this option. It is also vital that you set an expiry date on any block purchases and enforce it.

This model can also work for therapists – for example a block of six sports massage treatments. It works well for higher value items such as personal training sessions.

Other package options include pricing discounts for shared sessions. This doesn't work for all products but can be very effective for some. Using Pilates as the example:

One hour private one-to-one mat session	£55
One hour private duo mat session	£35 per person
One hour private trio mat session	£25 per person

Packages like this are popular with couples who want to train together and also for groups of friends.

It is important with shared sessions that you make it clear that if for example a trio session has been booked and only two of the three friends turn up, they must pay the 'duo' price.

Bundling packages are another way to offer good value to your customers and to sell a wider range of products. Let's use the example of an aromatherapy massage therapist. In this example the following three treatments are all available as stand-alone products from the rate card:

Indian head massage (20 min treatment)	£25
Back and shoulder Swedish massage (30 min treatment)	£35
Reflexology foot massage (30 min treatment)	£35
Complete Deep Relax Package	£75 (saving £20)

Memberships

Membership packages are very much the model used by the gym industry and it's tempting to think that this could be a good way forward if you are a sole trader in the fitness industry, for example as a Pilates, Yoga, Nordic Walking or group Fitness Teacher. I am not a fan of membership packages unless you have large premises with lots of classes on offer, which are not limited to relatively small numbers.

The Gym industry membership package works well because it is based on the assumption that a huge number of people will commit to a membership in January and then taper off and not use the facility that much. At the same time they will continue paying a direct debit that just ticks away in the background. They pay for the use of the gym even when they are away on holiday. Group class sizes in gyms tend to be large (thirty plus people in a class) so the per person cost is low. This is not the case for Yoga, Pilates and Nordic Walking classes, as they tend to be smaller.

We ran a membership scheme at Barefoot Studio for a few years. Members paid £72 a month for unlimited Pilates and Nordic Walking classes. To put this scheme in context, all of our classes are limited to twelve people per class. The people who took up our Barefoot Unlimited membership were all already committed attendees. When we analysed attendance, we saw that our members typically came to a class a minimum of three times a week and often four or five times a week. On average it worked out that they were paying £4.50 per class, a higher than 50% discount on the rate card charge for that class. It was common in many of the classes I taught for half of the people attending to be Barefoot Unlimited members. You can see how this would significantly skew the rate card calculation.

There is one more reason why memberships can be problematic for small fitness businesses, especially sole traders; holidays! Barefoot Studio offers fewer classes in the school holidays. If you work on your own, there may be no classes available to members when you are on holiday. We had complaints from the Barefoot Unlimited members that they had less choice of classes in the summer holidays yet were still paying the same monthly fee. We then had to schedule additional classes which ended up being poorly attended... I think you get the picture!

If you run a fitness business that is based around small classes, and especially if you are the only teacher, then I would avoid membership schemes. Obviously for therapists this model is not relevant at all.

By the end of this section you should have a good idea of your rate card or how to go about creating one. Your products should be clearly listed with pricing for individual sessions and set discounts for bulk purchases. The pricing should have been calculated taking into account the costs involved and with the value to the customer incorporated. Now you need to do some market research to check your pricing. Use the internet to check out similar businesses in your area and find out what they charge. You do not have to be cheaper, but you should be roughly in a similar price range. Make sure you are comparing like for like. So, for example, if you are a qualified Nutritional Therapist and you offer small group classes, checking out what a local slimming club charges would not be a fair comparison.

Healthy mind and body – healthy bank
Managing your business money

Now you have begun to monetise your business, you need to manage your business finances. You need to know whether you are on track to hit your income targets, whether your estimated operational costs were accurate and to know at any one time if you are profitable or not.

I share my office at Barefoot Studio with Jan, our marvellous Finance Officer. As well as working for us Jan does freelance book keeping and manages many of our therapists' End of Year returns. Every year there is a steady procession of therapists coming into the office with shoe boxes, carrier bags and scraps of paper, all saying 'Sorry Jan, it's a bit of a mess'. Some of them literally hand over a box rammed full of receipts and a copy of their bank statement showing what money they've banked that year. Jan works her magic and then tells them a few weeks later whether they actually made any money.

Knowing your bottom line on at least a monthly basis is one of the most essential business tools you can have. By following Step 2 MAP, you will have hopefully worked out exactly where you want to be in terms of income. You will also have set out a timescale for this, in effect setting yourself some targets. Managing your business money is the best tool you have for checking if you are on target or not.

These days there are many apps and software packages available to help you easily manage your business money. Some apps even let you snap a quick photo of your receipt on a smart phone which is then automatically pulled into your accounts. If you don't have a lot of transactions, then a simple spreadsheet is a good place to start. However you track money in and money out, you need to be able to work out how far you have travelled along your mapped out route to the income levels you desire.

For example, say you are a therapist charging £45 for a one hour counselling session. Your target is to make £20,000 a year in Year 1 and to be at this level of income within six months. Your annual fixed costs are about £2,000 which equates to £4.75 per session. It costs you £10 per session in 'cost of goods'. So, your profit is a little over £30 per session. To take £20,000 a year you would need to have fifteen paid sessions a week based on working forty-two weeks of the year.

On a monthly basis, this therapist should be asking the following questions:

- How many actual paid sessions did I have in the last month?
- Is this above or below where I should be at this point in my plan?
- Have my actual operational costs been the same as I budgeted or have I over/under spent?
- Have my costs per session been as I predicted or have there been any changes?

If the therapist is falling short on their targets, then they need to reflect on their marketing strategy and to look at what is working and what is not working in terms of getting new clients and keeping existing ones.

The better financial records you keep, the better you will be able to manage your business and the smaller your accountancy bill will be at the end of the year. Know that it is not an option to be ignorant of how your Health and Fitness business is performing financially. Knowledge is power.

Word of caution: on balance, it is also important to not get caught up in the minutiae of the finances on a day to day basis.

Make sure you step back and look at the bigger picture over a reasonable time frame, for example at the end of a teaching term, or quarterly.

Cancellation policies

Having a robust cancellation policy is a must for every Health and Fitness business. Not having a cancellation policy is probably the second biggest mistake that people make, after undercharging.

When I first started teaching Pilates I was very susceptible to a good cancellation 'sob story'. Sadly, what I have realised with time is that the more generous you are the more people take advantage of you.

Here is why a cancellation policy is essential.

Firstly, you have just calculated the true costs of running your business. Many of these costs are fixed whether people show up for their session or not. If someone cancels their session within a timescale that makes it unrealistic for you to fill their slot, then you have to bear the cost of those overheads. It is not a neutral financial situation.

Secondly, in many cases charging someone for their session when they cancel late can act as a motivator. Therapists in particular, but also fitness instructors, may be working with people who struggle to stay motivated or who on some level sabotage their own treatment or training plan. On those days when someone is thinking they might not bother to turn up, the thought of losing their money may be just enough of an incentive to get them to their session.

At Barefoot Studio we have a 100% of the fee twenty-four hour cancellation policy for all of our classes, one-to-one sessions and treatment rooms. All our clients receive email confirmation of their session and this contains a reminder of our cancellation policy. When people speak to someone on reception to make a booking the member of staff will remind them of our twenty-four hour cancellation policy. We are fairly strict on enforcing this. On rare occasions, we will waive it but this is very much the exception. People still ask if we will waive our cancellation charge for things like being stuck in work, stuck in traffic, childcare falling through etc. These days I always say no. It may feel harsh at first but remember you are running a business. The more you enforce this policy the clearer it becomes in your mind and in your customer's minds and the easier it becomes. I promise you that it is very rare that a client will complain about it. Especially if you clearly state your policy whenever there is a booking or monetary transaction. We have a copy of our cancellation policy on the wall and on the bottom of the studio timetable flyer.

Annual price increases

When I first opened Barefoot Studio, one of my clients, Patrick, gave me a really good bit of advice. He said to ensure that I increase my prices every January even if it is by a tiny amount. At first this didn't feel easy and I ended up with some odd prices like £7.50 for a class, but I trusted Patrick's advice and followed it every January.

I've spoken to so many therapists and Instructors who have charged the same fee for the services they provide for years and years. One therapist I spoke to had never increased her prices and she had been working for ten years! If you do this you are then faced with the prospect of either slowly making less and less money (as your costs go up each year) or suddenly having to make a big adjustment which is always received painfully by your customers. If you don't increase your charges each year you are also failing to reflect your growing body of knowledge and experience in your rate card.

DO! EXERCISE

▶ At the beginning of December every year I want you to diarise reviewing your rate card and fixing prices for the following Calendar Year. Then just put a note on the wall, or add a footer to your emails politely stating that from the 1 January your charges will be… This gives people four weeks' notice of the increase and it will make it easy for you to be able to ask for this additional charge when it is implemented.

Summary

Step 3 MONETISE is the crucial step that takes you away from being a hobby business or from running a charity and into earning a living. When you have clarity over your pricing structure and really understand the true costs of delivering the service you provide, you are far more likely to value what you do. If needed, you would be able to explain to someone why you charge what you do and why you have a cancellation policy.

For some people the most uncomfortable part of being in business is asking people for money. Having a clear rationale for what you charge will really help with this. Practise looking people in the eye and confidently telling them what you charge. You can ask someone to help you practise this. I once worked with a therapist called Sally who just couldn't tell people what she charged. She'd apologise to the client, splutter and mumble and then state some ridiculously low amount. I used to ring Sally up randomly throughout the day, pretending to be a customer and ask her what she charged for an initial consultation and follow up session. After a few days of this Sally became really good at explaining what she offered and what she charged in a matter-of-fact way.

Now you are starting to think like a business person. You have a clear vision of where you want to go and this is mapped out with key landmarks along the way. You understand how to make your business profitable and have a rate card that reflects the value of what you do and that ensures you earn a living wage. The next step is to get that phone ringing so you have people to explain your charges to!

Step 4 MARKETING is where you will hone your message and get it out to the tribe you identified in MAP.

CHAPTER SEVEN

MARKET

STEP
4

Market

The next step of the *Thrive* model is MARKET. If you have completed the **DO! EXERCISES** in the previous steps, you should have all the information you need to successfully market your Health and Fitness business.

You should now know:

1. Where you want to base your business geographically.

2. The level of income to which you aspire.

3. The times of day and frequency at which you want to work.

4. Who your tribe is, the time of day they are available to access your service and where they hang out.

5. The list of products you can offer and your rate card for every one of these products.

Now that you have identified who your tribe is and some of their behaviours, you are going to dive deep into their 'fears', I want you to really understand what problem(s) your tribe has that only you can solve. If you can communicate how your service can transform someone's 'fear' into a life that they 'love', then you will easily market your business. You are going to hone your key message and then decide which will be the most effective way to communicate this message to your tribe.

By the end of this section you will have designed a marketing action plan that will bring all this information together and give you a clear plan to work through.

Defining your message: selling what you do and not you!

As when deciding what to charge for your services, in marketing you must also place the emphasis on selling what you do and not just trying to sell yourself. To go back to my café analogy, think of yourself as the waitress bringing me my lovely cup of tea and not as the refreshing cup of tea itself! Remember it is the cup of tea and the way it makes me feel that the café markets, and not the waitress.

Let's start by reflecting on what made you become the therapist or health professional that you are today. Why do you love what you do? Why do you believe that it works?

DO! EXERCISE

▶ On a piece of blank paper draw two columns. The left column is the heartfelt 'feeling' side and the right column contains the hard facts. List as many reasons as you can under each heading:

| Why you love what you do | Why you know it works |

When you run out of steam in this exercise, review your lists and cluster together any similar items. Then circle the top three things you love about what you do and then the top three things you listed as to why you know it works. These six headline items are going to form the main part of the key message that you are going to send out to your tribe. From those six messages, is there any one message that really stands out for you?

Honing your message

Really successful businesses know their tribe and understand their key problems. Take your Tribe, as defined in Step 2 MAP, and put yourself in their mindset. Ask yourself:

- ◆ What are they concerned about?
- ◆ What would they like to change about themselves or their lives?
- ◆ What keeps them awake at night?

I will give you some examples. I provide specialist classes for people with long term chronic lower back pain. These are the problems that a typical member of this tribe face on a daily basis. These are some of their big fears:

- Constant pain
- Inability to do daily living tasks like cleaning the house, putting shoes on
- Not sleeping well
- Having to take high levels of pain medication
- Effect on their relationships with their families, e.g. can't play with the children/grandchildren
- Keep having to take time off, so worried they might lose their job
- Doctor offers only pain medication or surgery, neither appeal
- Giving up the things they love e.g. sport, gardening or travel
- Scared that if they go out their back may go into spasm and they will get stuck somewhere
- Becoming less active, experiencing more pain and trapped in a cycle
- Fear of damaging back even more and ending up in a wheelchair or needing surgery.

I could go on and probably fill a couple pages with more examples of what my typical lower back pain client is worried about. I bet you could come up with just as long a list of the worries, fears and hopes that your typical client has.

Once you have finished your long list of your clients' fears and problems then I want you to whittle it down to the big three issues in the same way that you pared down your list of *why you love what you do* and *why you know it works*.

Now imagine if you were one of my lower back pain clients and I could tell you a way to start to solve or manage these problems so that you can get back to enjoying life and moving again. I don't want you to exaggerate or make false promises. Refer back to your list of why you love what you do and why you know it works.

You should end up with three lists, each with your top three items underneath them:

Why you love what you do	Why what you do works	Your tribes problems/fears
1.	1.	1.
2.	2.	2.
3.	3.	3.

If there is a clear intersection between the service that you offer and your tribe's three biggest fears, then you have a clear and easy message to convey. If you really do love what you do and truly believe that it works, then your message will come across as authentic. Authenticity is essential to any good marketing strategy.

One way to convey the genuine nature of what you do is to use personal testimony. There is a lot of truth in the saying, 'stories sell'.

Capture stories

Whenever you can, you need to capture testimonials or case studies from clients who have benefitted from your services. You must check that people are happy for their stories to be shared. In my experience people are often delighted to do so because they ultimately want to help someone else in a similar situation who might also benefit from the services you offer.

Here is an example of a case study from my healthy back programme:

'I contacted Karen because my back pain was seriously affecting my life and I didn't know what else I could do. Six months previously I had been due to be married in Australia. Family and friends were flying out with me and my fiancé. My back problems got so bad that three weeks before the wedding we had to call it off. I was devastated. After a course of steroid injections I was getting better and so we had re-booked the wedding for the same time the following year. I was dreading the flight as sitting for any length of time caused me pain. I was still getting bad flair ups and was worried that I wasn't really addressing the cause of my back pain. I'd read that Pilates was good for backs and had also read about Karen's own personal story online. Karen started working with me on a one-to-one basis every week. She re-educated me to move from my deep postural muscles and to use my deep muscles to stabilise before I moved. She gave me exercises to do every day and homework each week. 'Scoop' became my new mantra, I scooped while I waited for the kettle to boil, I scooped when I stood up, I scooped when I got into the car. Slowly over time I got stronger and my back pain got less and less. Last week I had my dream wedding in Australia, standing on the beach. I can't thank Karen and Pilates enough'.

Emma, now living in
New Zealand with two children

There are lots of different ways to capture case studies, partly dependent on what type of Health and Fitness business you have. If it is appropriate one of the most powerful ways to do this currently is via video. It is easy to use a smart phone to record a quick visual interview with one of your case studies and to then share it with your tribe.

For the camera-shy, written testimonials can be very powerful. You could ask your case study to answer a short series of questions to help them structure their experience. For example:

1. What was the main reason you started coming to 'Amazing Therapy Solutions'?

2. What were the biggest challenges you were facing in your daily life and how did this make you feel?

3. What did you do on your programme with Amazing Therapy Solutions'?

4. How do you feel now and what has changed for you?

5. Would you recommend this approach to someone else facing similar issues to you?

If people are happy, it is lovely to support case studies with a photo. It makes the case study more real and human. This absolutely does not have to be a before and after type scenario!

Case studies and testimonials can be used on websites, in brochures, on social media and on flyers. They add authenticity to what you do and can be a powerful message. For therapists and movement teachers, a big part of what we do requires trust. Case studies can be an excellent way to start building trust with prospective clients.

As an example, here is my story...

My Story

I became a Pilates Instructor just over fifteen years ago and in many ways, Pilates saved my life, twice!

When I was twenty-one and a student, I had major surgery on my spine for two prolapsed discs. For the eighteen months before this surgery I'd been in agony and, once I'd recovered from the op it seemed to have been a miracle cure. I was pain-free and went straight back to sailing, skiing, cycling, all the things I loved. What I now know is that the surgery had done nothing to address the initial cause of my back problems – really bad muscle imbalance, rubbish postural muscles and glutes that did not fire... I officially had a lazy arse!

So, about five years later my back problems came back tenfold. I lost power and feeling in my left foot, had no reflex in my right ankle. It felt as if a spear had been thrust through my left calf. I couldn't work, in fact I couldn't do anything. I was advised to have a second operation but this time there was a risk of permanent damage and even paralysis. I was terrified. I decided to try everything before submitting to surgery. I tried massage, physio, chiropractic, osteo. I gave up cheese, had reiki... anything! Then I read an article about Pilates. My journey began.

After a couple of false starts, I found an excellent Pilates class and my road to recovery began. At the time there were few Pilates classes in Wales and I really wanted to learn more, so I enrolled on a course in London to train as a Pilates instructor.

As my body changed, my pain grew less and one day my spinal consultant said he no longer needed to see me. I was taken off the waiting list for surgery.

So that was how Pilates saved my life, the first time....

The second time? Even though I was getting stronger and stronger my day job was killing me. I worked in government policy and spent all day either at my desk writing strategies or in meetings. I realised I would never be 100% well unless I changed my job. After a week off work doing nothing but exploring movement on this amazing course, I was pain free and feeling alive. After one day back at my desk, I was back to being stiff and in pain. So I quit!

With my partner, we opened Barefoot Studio, the first Pilates studio and wellness centre in Wales. I taught Pilates and Nordic walking full time. We had a shop that sold many of the things that had helped me, like Swopper seating, healthy back bags, MBT footwear, plus we had a great team of therapists.

Pilates gave me a pain free life and one of the best jobs in the world. I work with people who've been dealt a similar hand to me and I teach them how to use Pilates to get their life back, too.

Thank you, Joseph Pilates!

Taking your message to your Tribe

By now you should have captured some key messages about why you love what you do, why you know it works and why your tribe needs you.

The next exercise I want you to do is to brainstorm a list of all the ways you could go out and tell people about what you do, why you love it and why it works. It is much easier to be creative with another person, so find someone you trust and share ideas. If you have set up a virtual team already, then you could use this group. At this stage I don't want you to censor your ideas. Assume that all ideas are good ideas, just write them down.

Here are some ideas to get you started:

- Put up a flyer in your local area
- Offer a taster session or talk to your local WI, Scout Group, book group etc
- Set up a Facebook page
- Invite a journalist to have a free session
- Have a stand at your local School/Village Fete or Agricultural Show
- Send out a press release to your local newspaper
- Advert in the Village or Parish magazine
- Attend a networking group
- Talk to your local GP surgery
- Offer a raffle prize or auction prize at a local charity fundraiser
- Offer a Team Building event
- Get listed on the Change for Life website
- (With permission) give out flyers at the school gates during the school run
- Contact U3A (University of the Third Age)

As you begin to brainstorm often one idea will lead to another. Try and capture everything you think of as you go along. If you can't write down the ideas quickly enough, then use your smart phone to record the discussion and type it up afterwards.

Hopefully, you will end up with a big long list of ideas. Now you need to match all these ideas with your Tribe.

Targeting your Tribe – matching your marketing ideas to your Tribe

In the last section I suggested that all ideas are good ideas. Well, they are not!

As small business owners, we often go down the DIY marketing route. This means that our ideas don't necessarily cost a lot of money but they often take a lot of time and effort.

I was once helping a newly qualified Nordic Walking Instructor come up with some ideas for marketing her classes. I asked her what she had tried in the past. She said she had got a couple of thousand flyers printed fairly cheaply for about £50, she had spent three full weekends, with her kids helping, pushing these through every letterbox in the small town where her classes were going to be running.

How effective do you think this was? What did you do with the last bit of 'junk mail' that was pushed through your letterbox? This marketing idea, whilst relatively cheap, took up a massive amount of time and probably yielded a very small response.

For every marketing idea you have, test it against these four measures:

1. What is the monetary cost?
2. What is the time and effort cost?
3. How big is the potential impact?
4. What is the time to market, i.e. how long will it take for your tribe to hear the message contained in your marketing idea?

So, in the example of my Nordic Walking instructor, her marketing idea analysis would have looked like this

1. LOW £50 for 2000 hits
2. HIGH 20+ hours
3. LOW probably less than 2% take up
4. IMMEDIATE people could respond within minutes of the flyer arriving

A good marketing plan needs a mixture of quick wins and long term slower burners. But, above all, it must hit your Tribe. Ultimately the Nordic Walking instructor was going very wide with a scatter gun approach rather than targeting her tribe.

Who buys Maltesers? Who buys Yorkies?

It is tempting to think that attracting anyone to your class or service is a good idea, but this approach is both expensive and random. For a moment imagine you are the marketing executive for Malteser. Take a moment to brainstorm your tribe:

Who eats Maltesers? Men or women? What age are they? What do they do for a living? Which newspaper or magazines do they read? Where do they go on holiday?

I bet your answers went something like this:

Women, 18-30, office workers who read Heat magazine and holiday in Ibiza!

Now, imagine you are the marketing executive for Yorkie:

Who eats Yorkie? Men or women? What age are they? What do they do for a living? Which magazines or newspaper do they read? Where do they go on holiday?

What did you come up with?

Men, 30+, truck drivers who read the Sun newspaper and go on holiday to Benidorm.

Harsh stereotypes I know, but you can be 100% sure that the marketing people at Mars (Malteser) and Nestle (Yorkie) know their Tribe. They can identify the 80% of their market who love their product. Of course, the makers of Malteser are delighted if men, and even male truck drivers, eat their chocolate, but this doesn't mean they are going to take out a full-page advert in *Truckers Weekly*. Likewise, Yorkie makers know that women eat their chocolate, but this doesn't mean that they are going to pay for a full-page advert in *Heat* magazine.

So now do this exercise matching up your marketing ideas with your tribe. Go back to the questions you asked yourself about your Tribe in MAP and the answers you came up with. Here is the list of questions that you used to define your tribe:

+ How old are they?
+ Are they men or women, or both?
+ Where do they hang out?
+ What do they like to read?
+ When is their free time?
+ What level is their disposable income?
+ What do they do for a living?
+ What hobbies or interests do they have?

DO! EXERCISE

▶ Now go back to your long list of marketing ideas and select the idea that you think will most specifically hit your target market or Tribe. Choose your top three ideas.

For example, my leaflet-dropping Nordic Walking instructor actually wanted to work with young mums wanting to lose weight after having kids. She wanted to work mornings, straight after the school run. We brainstormed many ideas and these ended up being the top three ideas that best aligned with her tribe:

1. Chatting with mums as they dropped their kids off (with the permission of the school). This idea further developed into running a free Nordic Walking taster session starting from the school and going into a nearby park. The session started at 9:15am straight after school drop off.

2. Offering an auction prize at the PTA's fundraising event. The prize was for a Nordic Walking session for the winning bidder plus nine friends. She wrote out some key messages for the auctioneer to read out and her prize was printed in the event programme.

3. To put up a poster in the café where lots of the mums met.

Once you have your top three ideas, stress test them against the following four measures:

1. What is the monetary cost?

2. What is the time and effort cost?

3. How big is the potential impact?

4. What is the time to market?

If you are happy with your top three ideas, then you need to specify a timescale for implementing them. You can then continue to prioritise your ideas using this method. Capture your whole Marketing Plan in a table and make sure you leave a column to note down how successful each idea actually was. I will explain more about this later.

Word of mouth - how to get your Tribe to recommend you

Word of mouth is a powerful marketing tool. Barefoot Studio has now been open for twelve years and our single biggest source of new clients for classes and therapists is word of mouth. We get referrals from happy customers and from other health professionals like Chiropractors, Osteopaths, Physiotherapists etc. We even get referrals for the Spinal Centre of Excellence at the local hospital. The phrase I see most regularly on our Client Enrolment Form in answer to the question, 'Where did you hear about Barefoot Studio?' is, 'From a friend'.

92% of consumers trust referrals from
people they know. 43% of consumers are more
likely to buy a new product when learning
about it from friends on social media.

{Neilson 'Trust in Advertising Report}

Ensuring you have happy customers is the best way to encourage word of mouth referrals. Think about the little touches you could add to the service that you offer to add a little 'sparkle' and make people feel really special. This can be as simple as making sure the environment you deliver your service in creates a good experience. For example,

I used to hire Village Halls and Community Centres when I first started teaching Pilates. It was very difficult to control who had used the room previously. I used to burn essential oils to make sure the room smelt nice as people entered. I provided the mats and head cushions and they all matched and looked professional. I made sure I knew all my client's names and greeted them by name as they entered and made lots of eye contact.

At Barefoot Studio, the philosophy of putting the customer at the heart of our business is one of the keys to our success. We do this in many small ways that individually people may not notice. However, together they make a strong impression. The principles that underlie all our customer interaction are respect and kindness, we really do go the extra mile to make our customers feel welcome.

Make happiness your business model: *What little things can you do on a daily basis to make your clients happy? Trade in happiness and in turn you will receive a top up of happiness back from your clients.*

When we set up Barefoot Studio, I went on a road trip to the USA to see as many mind-body spaces as I could. At that time there weren't many dedicated Pilates or Yoga wellbeing spaces in the UK. I asked everyone I met who owned the places I visited the same question, 'If you were opening your studio again which three things would be essential non-negotiables for you'. The top two answers were the same from every single person. The third varied but I made sure that Barefoot Studio would tick these first two things. They aren't very sexy but I promise you all those studio owners were right:

1. Make sure you have lots of easy and free parking

2. Make sure you have lots and lots of toilets

A friend of mine once joined a top end gym in the centre of Cardiff. It had state-of-the-art facilities, a gorgeous pool, lovely staff. It was perfect. After six months, she ended her gym membership despite a financial penalty. Why? The gym had a big car park but it was used by an office block as well. Often she would have to drive round and round the car park looking for a space and end up having to park a distance away in the street somewhere. She'd be late for her class and miss the first five minutes. Twice, she had her car broken into. She joined the gym to de-stress from her full-on job. In the end, using the gym just became too stressful. She never once recommended that gym to anyone.

One USA studio owner I spoke to was on the verge of moving to new premises. I couldn't understand why she was moving, her space was beautiful. A solid oak floor with under floor heating, beautiful light rooms, etc. 'Why?' I asked her. The answer was a surprise: 'I've only got one toilet'. Twelve or fifteen people would turn up for their Yoga class, all wanting a quick visit to the loo before class started. At the same time, the earlier class was emptying with clients wanting to use the toilet before going home. It caused long queues, class would start late and even then people would be wandering in five minutes after the class had begun because they'd been waiting to use the toilet! She was losing clients and no matter how good her product was, she was not getting any word of mouth referrals.

We spent six months looking for the premises that became the home of Barefoot Studio. No matter how stunning the place was, it was immediately struck off our short-list if it didn't tick those two boxes _ toilets and parking!

Reward people who refer

Most big gyms incentivise members to encourage their friends to also join the gym, with offers like, 'get a month's free membership when someone you refer joins'. For smaller Health and Fitness businesses, it's not always practical or desirable to make such big gestures. However, there are many small ways you could think of to reward customers who recommend you.

Hopefully, you have all had that special client who turns into your Number One Fan. They recommend you to everyone and generate a lot of business for you. If this person is the centre of a big social network, they are like gold. In his book *The Tipping Point*, Malcolm Gladwell referred to such people as 'Connectors'.

Connectors are the people in a community who know large numbers of people and who are in the habit of making intro-ductions. A connector is essentially the social equivalent of a computer network hub. They usually know people across an array of social, cultural, professional, and economic circles, and make a habit of introducing people who work or live in different circles. They are people who 'link us up with the world... people with a special gift for bringing the world together'. They are 'a handful of people with a truly extraor-dinary knack for making friends and acquaintances'.

If you have connectors in your client base, then you need to nurture them and make sure they stay your Number One Fan.

A massage therapist might offer a client who frequently refers, a one-off free session, just as a way of saying thank you. A Pilates teacher could reward a Connector with a free one-to-one Reformer session. Or more simply you could give your 'Connector' a gift. For example, an M&S Gift voucher or some flowers. Barefoot Studio also has a retail space where we sell clothing, accessories, props, socks, etc. If one of my Connectors picks up something at the end of their class and comes to pay for it and it's a low value item I might say, 'You can have that on me today as a thank you for referring Tom'.

Get to know your connectors. If a new client puts on their Enrolment Form that they heard about you 'from a friend', then ask them for the identity of that friend. Make sure you thank the 'Connector' when you next see them. If the same name keeps popping up, then make sure you become **their** Number One Fan in return.

Five secrets to making social media work for you

Social media is such a big part of marketing these days that it must have a role in your marketing plan.

According to the Office of National Statistics, the internet was used daily or almost daily by 82% of adults (41.8 million) in Great Britain in 2016[1]. In 2017, it is estimated that there will be around 35.7 million social network users in the UK[2].

The topic is huge and can feel overwhelming. It is easy for it to become massively time consuming and stressful. If you are not a savvy social media user then the following five tips will help you make a start:

 Choose just one social media platform to start with and focus solely on that. You are better off doing a good job on one platform than scattering yourself thinly over four or five of them. Facebook is still probably the biggest and most widely used. It's well suited to Health and Fitness businesses and it is relatively simple to set up a business page.

 Be careful of mixing business and pleasure. If possible, separate your personal social media presence from your professional one. Keep personal posts within a closed 'friends and family only' setting. Then make sure your business posts

---

1   Office of National Statistics: Statistical Bulletin: Internet Access – households and individuals 2016: published August 2016.
2   United Kingdom; eMarketer; 2014 to 2018; Internet users who use a social network site via any device at least once per month.

are professional. Only post based on what you want to be known for. Avoid expressing strong opinions on politics or being negative or disrespectful of others. Remember how personal and bitter social media posts became at the time of Brexit. You will lose customers if you launch into strong views on either side of contentious issues. You definitely don't want pictures of you out partying with your mates looking drunk! Post only in office hours – this creates a professional image and will also help you stay sane. We will look at this more in the last section on sustaining a healthy and profitable Health and Fitness business.

 Having said that, don't be too clinical – build relationships. Think carefully about what you want to convey with your social media. What are your values, what are your business values? A great place to start with this is to go back to your three lists of 'why you love what you do', 'why you know it works' and 'what your tribe needs'. You can use social media to show your prospective clients that you 'walk the talk', that you live this aspirational healthy and fit life. So it is absolutely okay to share pictures of you out walking with your dog or finishing a 10k run or of the lovely, healthy lunch you just made. Share an article about why drinking water is so good for you. Share your struggles too. Make yourself human, people will love you for it.

Use strong visual content – search engines and social media users absolutely love visual content. Social media is bombarded with millions of posts every minute, you need your posts to stand out in this busy market place. Adrian Stone is a success-ful film maker who uses short films on social media to incredible effect. I'd never used video clips much on social media, I didn't really know where to start. Adrian challenged me to make a quick video of anything to do with my business using my smart phone. I wasn't to edit it, just post it up and see what happened. I made a two-min-ute video of Barefoot Studio by slowly wandering from room to room, starting at the front door and ending in the second Pilates studio. It was a bit shaky and ended a bit abruptly and may well have made some people feel slightly sea sick. However, despite its faults, that video clip had more views and shares in one day than anything I had ever put up on Facebook. Unsurprisingly, Adrian was right. If you are really brave, dive into the world of Facebook Live! This is growing in popularity and can be very effective.

 Be consistent – a common mistake that many of us make with social media is that it is 'feast or famine'. I have been guilty of this in the past. One day or one week I post like mad, tweet away, put up photos, write a blog post... Then nothing for weeks. Consistency is everything. Work out a schedule for social media that is realistic and achievable. For example, one tweet a day, three Facebook posts a week and one blog article a month. Go for quality content rather than quantity and put your sched-ule in your diary. For example, commit to publish a blog article on the first Monday of every month and to always post on your business Facebook page every Monday and every Friday. If you are having a creative day, then you can sit down and prepare social media posts for the week in one sitting. You can then use apps like Hootsuite to automatically post the articles at the scheduled times you've planned.

Match your social media to your Tribe

There are so many choices of social media platforms that you could access. At the time of writing these were the most used, in order of popularity:

Facebook, YouTube, Twitter, Instagram, Google+, Pinterest, Snapchat, LinkedIn

When choosing which social media channels to focus your energies on refer back to your Tribes demographic. Choose the social media channel that best matches. This form of media moves so fast it is worth seeking out the latest statistics on who uses social media. Below are the demographics at the time of writing in 2016.

Facebook is still the leading social network with over 32 million users in the UK alone.

- Used equally by men and women.
- Although slightly more people under the age of 35 use Facebook, in 2016 the numbers of people using Facebook across all ages was fairly even
- Half of 18-24 year olds wake up and check their timeline
- Best days to post are Thursdays and Fridays. You get most shares at 1pm and most clicks at 3pm

YouTube is used by just over 19 million people in the UK

- More men than women use YouTube with 62% male users
- The most popular channels are music related

Twitter has 15 million active users in the UK

- Used equally by men and women
- 65% are under the age of 34
- Wednesday to Sunday are the most effective days to tweet to target customers with highest engagements on the weekends. 5pm is the best time for retweets

Instagram has 14 million active users in the UK, it has a much younger profile than Facebook

- 90% are under 35
- 39% of UK users are aged 16-24 years old.

Google + is used by 12.6 million people in the UK

- 63% of users are male and 37% female
- 41% of users are aged between 18-24 and 29% between 25-34
- The best time of day to post is between 9am and 11am on a weekday

Pinterest has 10 million users in the UK. Recipes are one of the top topics for UK Pinterest users, 46% having searched for this subject.

 • 62% of users are women

 • 70% of all users go on to act in some way on the content they find.

 • Mums are 3x more likely to share a pin than other users

 • Saturday is the best day of the week to Pin between 8pm and 11pm

LinkedIn is still the business to business social network leader. It has 10 million users in the UK

 • Male dominated, 80% of users are men, 20% women

 • 45% of active users are in higher management

 • Tuesdays, Wednesdays and Thursdays are the best days to post and the best time is during business hours.

There are also lots of analytics tools available to work out the best time of day to post so that it coincides with when your Tribe will be using social media.

How do you know which of your marketing ideas work the best?

It is really important that you track what works and what doesn't work in terms of marketing. It is amazing how soon we forget, if we don't record it, what is effective. There are two great ways to do this:

1. Most Therapists and Fitness Instructors have some type of Client Enrolment Form. Make sure you add two questions to the end of this form:

   A. How did you hear about _____ (insert name of treatment or type of fitness class you offer)?

   B. How did you hear about me or _____ (insert business name)?

2. On every marketing tactic that you use make sure there is a trackable 'Call to Action'.

The first method of monitoring what works is simple. Every time you get a new client, you can see what brought them to you. After a few weeks and months, you will see patterns emerging. If you spend £100 on a paid advert in your local newspaper and you never have anyone answer question B with 'Advert in the Echo newspaper', then you know you wasted your money. If you are good at what you do, in time the most frequent answer to this question will be 'word of mouth'.

The second method, using a 'Call to Action' is equally important. This can help you in two ways. Firstly, to track what has worked but just as importantly, to galvanise someone into acting on the marketing they have seen.

Here are some examples of 'Calls to Action'

Campaign: advert in the Parish magazine for six weeks Beginners Pilates Course
Call to Action: quote 'Parish Mag' when you book to get £5 off the course

Campaign: Poster campaign in local Coffee Shop
Call to Action: quote 'Coffee shop' when you book and get two places for the price of one

Campaign: At a Health Promotion Event give out cards or flyers
Call to Action: claim a free spinal health check 'with this card'

The principle of a Call to Action is that the person has to quote the marketing source when they book in order to generate some sort of saving or offer. In this way you can track exactly how many new customers stemmed from a specific poster or advert etc.

If you continue to monitor and record the outcome of every marketing action you will build up a good picture of what works for you and your Tribe.

I use a simple spreadsheet to track what works and what doesn't.

These are the headings I use:

* Name of marketing promotion I carried out: e.g. Poster campaign
* Brief description: e.g. Posters advertising January Beginners Course in ten local shops and café
* Cost: Actual cash it cost, in this example I printed the posters on my computer, so negligible cost

- Time: two hours to display the posters
- Date it went to market: The actual date your audience will see the marketing, e.g. the weekend of 1 December
- Outcome: This is the most important column. In this example I would check my client enrolment forms in January and see how many people said they saw a poster

This simple spreadsheet will help you keep on track and not waste time or money on ineffective strategies. If you do go down the route of paid advertising, it is even more important that you know if the advert you took out had an impact.

Advertising sales people are brilliant at ringing you and using this kind of sales pitch:

'Hi Karen, its Jenny from *Ladies First* magazine. We're just about to run the January Health and Fitness feature again. You took out a half page advert in this last year and had such an amazing response. I've still got your artwork and will hold last year's price. So it's just £600. Shall I book you in?'

Before I tracked my marketing, I would probably have been unable to recall how effective the advert had been and would just say yes. These days I get out my spreadsheet, see that the advert only generated three bookings and would say no thank you!

Summary

We've explored the Market, Message and Media elements of Step 4 MARKET, and you are beginning to know your Tribe inside and out. You know what makes them tick, where they hang out, what they read, and what keeps them up at night. You've honed your message so that it speaks directly to this market. You've captured stories and case studies that humanise your message and give inspirational examples of why what you do works. You've brainstormed a good list of marketing ideas of where and how you can shout out your message. You've then refined this list to make sure that your message, media and tribe all align for the best impact. We've also looked at how you can capitalise on word-of-mouth referrals and ways to get started with social media.

As this all starts to take effect your phone will start ringing, the emails will start landing and your diary will start to fill up with busy classes and booked sessions. The next challenge is how to manage your busy business.

Before we start to look at Step 5 MANAGE, I want to end this by sharing a story with you.

I had a fifteen-minute break between 1-2-1 clients and happened to be on the Studio reception desk when the phone rang. I answered the call and it was a new customer who wanted to book in for a 1-2-1 Reformer Pilates session with me. They'd been recommended to me by a friend who had raved about Barefoot Studio and what Pilates had done for them. I pulled up my schedule and searched for an appointment. And then it struck me, I was fully booked and would be for weeks! I had to explain to the person that I was sorry that I was fully booked and had no openings for new clients. They could either join the waiting list or they could book in with one of our other teachers. Luckily, they did the latter. Next week I was in session with the client who had referred this friend. She said how happy her friend was with the session she'd had with my colleague. She then puffed herself up slightly and proudly commented that she was delighted that she was one of my clients.

I'm now regularly oversubscribed for my private 1-2-1 appointments. It's a wonderful feeling when people start chasing you and you can stop chasing them. A pleasant side effect of being oversubscribed is that my clients never complain when I inform them of my annual fee increase.

Get your marketing strategy right and you will create a buzz around what you do. When being busy is based on a sound pricing structure then you also become profitable.

The next step is to MANAGE your business in a way that minimises stress and keeps your business enjoyable and fun!

CHAPTER EIGHT

Manage

Until now we have been focusing on the profitable side of running a Health and Fitness business. In MINDSET I talked about how to start thinking like a business person and how to change your thinking so that you understand that making money out of what you do is a good thing. In MAP we set out a clear picture of where you want to be in terms of lifestyle and income levels. We've identified your market or Tribe and identified their problems and how you are going to solve these problems. In MONETISE I explained how to correctly charge for what you do. You should now be able to put a price on what you do that's realistic and reflects the true value of your skills and expertise. In MARKET we honed your message and shouted it loud and clear right into the ear of your tribe. When this all works together, your business will take off and you will start to generate a good income.

The final piece of the jigsaw puzzle, and Step 5 of the *Thrive* model, is MANAGE. The busier you get the more the admin burden of the business grows, particularly if you've not yet hit the tipping point of being able to employ someone to help. A well-managed business is a happy business. I know you love what you do when you are with a client, you value and prioritise this aspect of the business above all else. However, it is how you schedule and manage the day-to-day operational tasks that in many ways makes being in business a pleasure, or a pain.

In this chapter, we are going to look at time management and dealing with competing priorities. I'm going to talk you through the concept of maintaining office hours and allotting times when you are unavailable. I also want to address the issues we explored when I talked about Lone Worker Syndrome by helping you to develop a Support Network or Virtual Team. Too many sole traders experience burn out and this step, MANAGE, is all about avoiding that so that you keep enjoying your job. This is the **happy** bit of the 'secret to a happy and profitable business.'

Time management – setting 'office hours' – it's OK to be unavailable

On a Friday morning a few months ago, I contacted a number of website development companies as we were planning to redevelop our website. I'd done a bit of research and drawn up a shortlist of companies I liked. As you'd expect they all had really professional websites and looked like fairly big companies. I emailed the five companies I shortlisted with an outline of what we were looking for and asked them to email me back with a proposal.

On Sunday evening at about 10 pm I was just plugging my phone into charge when an email arrived from one of the website companies I'd contacted. It was a short very informal email, saying something like 'what you want is right up our street, yeah I'd love to work with you, ring me in the morning and I can talk you through some options' No email footer, just 'sent from my iPhone'.

Now, I could have thought, wow this is a hard-working guy emailing me at ten o'clock at night on a Sunday, he must be really good. What I actually thought was, wow – why is he emailing me on the weekend. This seems a bit chaotic, maybe this company is just a one-man band and he's over-stretched and having to do his admin on a Sunday night. He was crossed off my shortlist.

For me it is essential that you set fixed business hours as much as you possibly can and stick to them. My reasons for this are twofold:

1. It will help you manage your time and help you to switch off. If you give yourself permission to check emails late into the night, then the working day gets longer and longer and you have too little down time.

2. It gives a clear and professional message to both existing and prospective customers. I think this is particularly relevant to Health and Fitness based businesses where we have to be especially mindful of boundaries. You don't want to create the impression that it is OK for your clients to ring you on your mobile on the weekend because something came up.

In the 'good old days', we all got up in the morning, ate breakfast and then went into work. At the end of the day the answer phone was switched on and we all went home. I knew that if I rang most businesses after 5:30 pm in the evening I would get an answer phone and if I was lucky the message would be listened to at 9:00 am the following morning.

All of this has changed with many very successful businesses now run without premises, just a mobile phone, a website and email. The danger with this model of business is that we make ourselves open for business 24/7.

Here are some tips for managing this:

- Set up an auto reply 'out of office message' on your email that thanks the person for their email, states your business hours and tells them when to expect a response. Some email packages will let you set this up so it comes on automatically at fixed times. You could simply activate it at the end of the day when you have finished work if you don't have this facility.

- Use the caller ID function and only answer your phone to friends and family outside of your fixed business hours. When you don't know who the caller is, let it go to voicemail. Make sure you have a professional voicemail message that you have recorded yourself that clearly states your business hours.

- A good friend of mine, Helga Sylvester, runs a hugely successful Pilates studio in Rotterdam, The Pilates Place. Helga does have a landline in the studio and a receptionist who takes calls, but she also uses a mobile for her business. She actually carries two mobile phones with her. One is for personal contacts and the other is business only. This is a great solution. She can switch the work phone off at the end of the business day and she knows all calls are picked up by her voicemail. As she has a personal phone too she knows that all important personal calls will get through. This method also ensures that her clients do not have her personal contact details.

The key to the success of any of these systems is to ensure you make good on your promises. So, if your voicemail message or auto email reply says you will respond within a certain time frame, then make sure you do so.

The same rules apply for social media direct messaging. Implement similar professional boundaries to these.

Finally, don't be afraid to be shut. Take at least one complete day a week off, make 'I don't work Sundays' your new religion. This doesn't just mean have no client contact on Sundays, it means have a totally business-free day.

Dealing with competing priorities

Who knew that running your own Pilates studio would mean you were the cleaner, receptionist, IT expert, marketer, teacher, maintenance person, finance officer, secretary, admin person, web mistress...

In many ways the easy bit is the set service delivery hours. The hours when I teach Pilates are fixed in advance and are non-negotiable. It would be much easier if the other aspects of the job were also fixed.

I have tried lots of different approaches to managing the varied tasks of running a business and in the following section I summarise some of the ones that worked best for me. All the following examples are manual systems. I will go on to talk about some of the amazing electronic tools that are now available.

Fixed time slots for specific tasks

Multi-tasking doesn't really work. We just end up being inefficient and wasting time. In the same way that your face-to-face sessions are set in the diary, it can work if you schedule chunks of time for specific tasks

Chunking is an actual time management tool and it is really simple.

1. Identify some broad headings for your weekly tasks, for example: session planning, marketing, writing a blog, following up enquiries, etc.

2. Allocate a 'chunk' of time to each task based on how long you think it will take.

3. Commit times in your weekly schedule to each of these chunks.

4. While you are working on a chunk you must not look at emails, answer the phone, etc. Do not deviate until you have finished the task at hand.

After a bit of practice and discipline, this technique can work really well.

Colour-coded diaries

I use an electronic diary which is synced across all my devices so I can access it on my laptop or phone, at work or at home. Colour coding also works well on a paper diary as long as you always have some coloured pens to hand.

Key sections and tasks associated with my business are allocated a colour. So, for example, for writing this book I allocated the colour Hot Pink. Financial tasks might be red. Teaching slots are blue in my diary, staff related issues are yellow. By writing in your diary in these different colours, you can see at a glance what your week or day is looking like. You can also block out half days or blocks of time in a colour so that you know that afternoon is committed to working on the website, for example.

Pomodoro technique

My publisher, Lucy McCarraher, recommended this method to me when I was writing this book. It is really simple and perfect if you are easily distracted or procrastinate. The method is named after the tomato-shaped kitchen timer, the Pomodoro, you can buy. It works by focusing on a single task for twenty-five minutes at a time (I call these sprints) and then taking short breaks.

There are six steps in the technique:

1. Decide on the task to be done.

2. Set a timer (traditionally to twenty-five minutes). I just use the timer on my phone.

3. Work on the task until the timer rings. If a distraction pops into your head, write it down, but immediately get back on task.

4. After the timer rings, put a tally mark on a piece of paper to mark off the completion of one 'sprint'. Take a short three-to five-minute break.

5. Then set the timer again and work for another twenty-five minutes on either the same task or, if it is finished, a new task. Repeat steps 1 to 4 until you have completed four sprints.

6. After four sprints, take a longer break (fifteen to thirty minutes), reset your checkmark count to zero, then go back to step 1.

You can find out more about this method at www.pomodorotechnique.com

My little black books

Use a notebook – one strategy that many organised people use is to work with a notebook. This notebook is like a 'catch-all' for your thoughts and for what you do during the day. I always have one moleskin notebook on the go. My past editions are lined up on a shelf in my office and they go back years and years.

I use my notebook to take notes when I'm talking with a colleague or with a client on the phone. If I'm busy working on a scheduled task and something pops into my head, my notebook is always right there and I can record the thought or task to refer back to later. If I find myself having a creative moment, then I can capture it in the notebook.

The advantage of a notebook is that you keep all of your thoughts, conversations, and ideas in one place. And, once things are written down, you don't have to waste mental energy remembering everything! I always write Today's Date in the notebook and when the book is full I write the start and finish date for that book inside the front cover before it goes up on the shelf with the others. This way, you can easily go back and find the information you need.

To-do lists and weekly planners

To-do lists can work really well but once you have your list you must rank it in order of importance. Then, if you want to you can be really effective and use the chunking technique to get through the tasks.

I use a traffic light system by assigning every item on my to do list with a RAG status – red, amber or green:

STOP there's no need to do this just yet, but you need to find time to do this task soon

GET READY you need to get this done soon, but not necessarily today

GO, GO GO, you need to get this done today

Just circle round each task on your to do list with a coloured pen so you can decide how to prioritise your list. Then chunk your time and tick them off your list.

Using technology – how to manage your business wherever you are

There are many fantastic tools on the market that make it possible for you to run your business from your mobile from anywhere in the world.

You can use integrated software to manage your diary, finances, contacts, communications and even your social media.

You don't have to buy such software like this outright, as most is available for a monthly fee. At first glance you may be tempted to say you can't afford to sign up for a monthly subscription. However, this fee is likely to equate to only a few hours of your time a month in terms of income and could save you hours and improve efficiency. Tasks can become more streamlined and you are less likely to miss leads or miss deadlines.

When we first opened Barefoot Studio, we managed all of our class bookings using paper. People bought a Class Pass and we gave them a card with numbers on which we hole punched each time they came to class. A few years in and we invested in professional studio management software. It seemed a lot of money at the time but it gave us some invaluable data. This included how we were performing, our client's profiles, and the profitability of different classes. The most immediate and obvious benefit was how the software managed our twenty-four-hour cancellation policy. No more having to listen to late cancellation sob stories, the computer just said no!

Whichever task management tools work for you, make sure that you allocate time for the essential business tasks. Little and often is the key.

Building a support network and virtual team

Earlier, we explored the Lone Worker Syndrome and the challenges that sole traders can face running everything alone. The best solution for this is to build your own Support Network or a Virtual Team.

There are a few ways to do this:

Local support team

Do you know up to four local people who would be willing to meet with you monthly to act as a voluntary 'Advisory Board'? They don't have to be connected to the Health and Fitness industry. They could be other business owners, good at finance, or creative thinkers, for example. Above all, you have to trust them.

You need to make the group reasonably formal. Agree an agenda for your meetings and clear terms of reference for the group. Also, make it clear that it is voluntary and that ultimately it is your business. The deal could be that you meet over lunch and that you pay for the lunch. You work for an hour discussing your business and then you do something fun together. I've helped out a couple of friends in this way and it can be hugely rewarding.

When I worked in the voluntary sector this was a model that was used, albeit much more formally, to great effect. Your group can act as a sounding board, focus group, mini market research, creative ideas generator, problem solver and most importantly to provide that feeling of team and support for you. For example, once you have worked through the 5 Ms of the *Thrive* model, you could present your conclusions and ideas to your Advisory Board for feedback. Do they agree with your assumptions about your Tribe? What do they think about your rate card? Can they come up with more ideas for marketing?

When you are in the start-up phase of your business you may want to meet fairly frequently. Thereafter you might only want to meet six times a year. The nice thing about working with people you know and trust is, you can always turn to them when you need them.

Virtual Teams

The internet has brought us much closer and there are many professional forums on platforms like Facebook into which you can tap. I belong to a couple of Pilates Teacher Forums where I can post questions about a particular injury I've come across or ask for class ideas, for example. Often groups like this can have members from all around the world. They can be an incredible resource into which you can tap.

You can also set up your own groups. I do this with my trainee Pilates Teachers so that they can keep in touch with each other and support one another as they start to run classes and set up their businesses. People on my Business Support Programme are put into 'buddy groups' so that they can work together and support each other as they grow their businesses.

The underlying principle of all Virtual Teams like this is that you have to give in order to get. It is very much about offering support as well as receiving it, sharing your best ideas and receiving other people's ideas in return.

Get a Business Mentor

The top option for all small business owners is to find a good Business Mentor. This can be especially beneficial in the start-up phase of a business but even on an ongoing basis it will keep you focused and moving forward. If you lack skills in one area of business management, then your mentor can help you learn these skills.

I have used mentors throughout my time in business. When we first opened Barefoot Studio we were fortunate to have a business mentor who was paid for by the Welsh Government. He helped us with practical tasks like writing Business Plans and asked us searching questions to help guide our thinking and planning. Five years later we used a business mentor to help us develop a new retail project and to guide us through a period of growth. The benefits of working with a mentor always more than justify the costs.

I now offer Business Mentoring as part of my work with Health and Fitness Practitioners. It is a hugely rewarding part of my job.

Professional forums

You will find there is a wealth of local groups that you could join. For example, within a five-mile radius of Barefoot Studio there are two Chambers of Commerce, a Women in Business Forum, a Business Breakfast Club and probably others. Getting involved in such groups offers good networking opportunities. They often have Guest Speakers who will be able to bring you up to date on changes in legislation that may affect your business, or funding opportunities, for example. Plus, you have a ready-made sounding board for ideas.

Sub-contract out

I have wasted so much time over the years struggling on my own to do a task for which I didn't really have the skills. A good example of this would be websites. I've built a couple of our websites and the task sucked up too much of my time. If I'd paid someone to do it for me, it would have been a lot more efficient and considerably better. Whenever you can, stick to the jobs you are good at and where your skills lie and, as soon as you can afford to, buy in help for the areas that are not part of your skills set. By building up a list of local people whose services you can buy in, you will build up a team that you can use whenever you need them.

Over time you will probably find that your Support Team is drawn from a few of the ideas above. Whichever way you build your team around you, do build one. All successful businesses need a team, especially if they also want to be happy businesses.

'Be a friendly professional not a professional friend'

I love this saying. In some therapies, like counselling, there are clear professional Codes of Ethics that cover the line between someone starting out as a client and becoming a friend or even preventing a friend from becoming a client. For many other Health and Fitness businesses the distinction is not so clear cut.

For most people, it is much easier to manage your business if you keep your client relationships on a professional footing. There are wonderful, fascinating people that come to Barefoot Studio, I've got to know some of them very well. Sometimes I wonder if I am a counsellor as well as a Pilates Teacher. We have social get-togethers like the Barefoot Studio Christmas Party or a Summer Nordic Walk to the pub. Barefoot Studio is a very friendly place, but it doesn't mean that our customers are also our friends. Conversely, my personal friends are not customers.

Of course, on occasion, you really 'click' with someone and they might cross this line. When this happens, though, it can become difficult to also maintain a professional relationship. An expectation of 'mate's rates' can suddenly pop up, or there is an assumption that the twenty-four-hour cancellation policy no longer applies to them, or they start asking for lots of advice for which you would normally charge. Wherever possible keep clear professional boundaries and avoid muddying the waters.

One part of maintaining professional boundaries is *confidentiality*.

Again, some professional bodies have clear policies on confidentiality to which their members must adhere. This is true for practices like Counselling and Hypnotherapy, but also for manual therapies or fitness teachers who gather medical information on their clients.

I never discuss anything a client tells me with anyone, whether they tell me it in confidence or not. No matter how mundane the piece of news might be, you never know who knows who. It is unprofessional to gossip.

Summary

We've now explored the key areas of success-fully managing a happy business:

- Set your office hours
- Get organised
- Get support
- Be professional

Complete the following **DO! EXERCISE** check list and put the measures in place immediately, this will make sure you use your time wisely and efficiently manage your business so that you enjoy it.

DO! EXERCISE

▶ Take a moment to set your office hours. Work out exactly when you will be 'open'.

Put this information in your email footer and on your website so that the message is clear. Please, please, please include 'We are closed on Sundays'!

Start to explore support group options and set up something that you can tap into on a regular basis.

PART THREE

Sustaining a Happy and Profitable Lifestyle Business

'Gross National Happiness (GNH) is more important than GDP. The understanding of what humans need to make them happy is vital to our society'

Jigme Singye Wangchuck
His Majesty, the Fourth King of Bhutan

Looking to the Future

I hope you can now see how the *Thrive* model of the 5 Ms gives a clear process for you to follow.

By working through these five steps you should now:

- Be starting to think like a business person.

- Understand that it is a good thing to be profitable and that it is what you deserve.

- Have mapped out a clear plan for where you want to be with your business and at whom your business is targeted. You are beginning to know your Tribe inside and out, what makes them tick, where they hang out, what they read, and what keeps them up at night.

+ Have worked out your rate card and what your breakeven is for every service you deliver thereby ensuring that your business is profitable.

+ Have honed your message so that it speaks directly to your market. You've come up with lots of great marketing ideas and refined them down to the one that will hit your tribe hardest.

+ Organised your business so that it works for you. You know how to create a Support Team and how to manage your time and tasks.

The 5 Ms of the *Thrive* model unpack the secret to a happy and profitable Health, Wellbeing and Fitness business. I encourage you to work through all of the **DO! EXERCISES** and to keep reviewing and revisiting the Sections to help keep you on track.

In Part Three, we are going to look to the future. I'm going to talk about sustaining your business and, most importantly, sustaining you. I want you to have a great business but not at the cost of your own health and happiness. I don't just want your business to thrive, I want you to thrive too.

CHAPTER NINE

Be Happy

▼

In Part One of this book, we looked at the pitfalls and problems of running your own Health and Fitness business including the many challenges that we face and our deep held beliefs that hold us back.

In Part Two we identified the solution, a clear five step process you can adopt to run a successful business that is also profitable and fun.

In Part Three, I want to address the bigger promise of the title of this book, the happy bit!

When I first gave up a salaried job to set up my Pilates business there were both push and pull factors. I was good at my job but it was stressful, there was a whole load of politics involved and it was draining. It had stopped fulfilling me and it was making me unhappy. I'm sure like many of you, I wanted to run my own business so that I was the mistress of my own destiny and as a way of seeking a happier way to earn a living.

There certainly was a 'honeymoon period' where I relished the 'freedom' of being able to work when and where I wanted, in a positive environment, delivering a service that people wanted. The joy and the problem was that the business grew. In a relatively short period of time I had premises, a shop, staff and big scary overheads. I found myself declining invitations to meet up with friends because I was working. I don't think I had ever worked so many hours in my life. I had lost all balance and although I still loved what I did, I can't honestly say that I was happy.

I want to share some practical ideas of how to make sure this doesn't happen to you, so that you can keep relishing what you do and avoid burnout. Before I do this, I want to share a little of the philosophy that underpins Barefoot Studio.

Barefoot Studio has a mission statement, which is:

'Life is a journey full of movement and we want you to enjoy every minute of the ride'

Our business values are based upon the work of Don Miguel Ruiz and his book, *The Four Agreements*, which for many people is a life-changing book. The philosophy comes from the ancient Toltec wisdom of the native people of Southern Mexico. The Four Agreements of the book, as well as applying to an individual, make the perfect value base for Barefoot Studio.

Agreement 1

'Be impeccable with your word - Speak with integrity. Say only what you mean. Avoid using the word to speak against yourself or to gossip about others. Use the power of your word in the direction of truth and love.'

At Barefoot Studio we don't make false promises, we respect the privacy of our clients and we don't gossip about them. If you ask any of our team a question, you will get a straight answer. We run our business with integrity, we source our products ethically, pay our staff properly, and only sell products and services that we would use ourselves and that we know work. If someone comes into Barefoot Studio who is clearly looking for something that we can't help them with, then I refer them to someone else. I don't try and 'spin' what we do to fit with what they are asking for.

Agreement 2

'Don't take anything personally – Nothing others do is because of you. What others say and do is a projection of their own reality, their own dream. When you are immune to the opinions and actions of others, you won't be the victim of needless suffering.'

When you run a business based on your own personal values and based on something you are passionate about, it is really easy to take everything personally. When a client doesn't come back you take it personally and blame yourself. If your class is quiet one week, your first thought is, 'Did I do something wrong?', rather than, 'I wonder if there is something on at the school tonight?'. If someone questions how much you charge for something and suggests it should be cheaper, you take it as a reflection of you and your worth. I've talked to many Therapists and Fitness Teachers who torture themselves daily with these kind of thoughts. This is exhausting and futile.

Agreement 3

'Don't make assumptions - Find the courage to ask questions and to express what you really want. Communicate with others as clearly as you can to avoid misunderstandings, sadness and drama. With just this one agreement, you can completely transform your life.'

I would add to this statement, you can completely transform your business. Communicating clearly is the key to a happy business. If you are not clear what someone is asking for, then ask them questions until you are clear. If conflict comes up, deal with it immediately without making assumptions and by being impeccable. We work with an incredible variety of people from every walk of life. It is important that you don't make assumptions about someone just by the way they look, or what they wear or how they speak. Work with people based on what you actually know about them and not on what you have assumed.

Agreement 4

'Always do your best - Your best is going to change from moment to moment. It will be different when you are healthy as opposed to sick. Under any circumstance, simply do your best, and you will avoid self-judgment, self-abuse and regret.'

The whole thrust of this agreement is about doing your best. This doesn't mean bending over backwards to accommodate everyone. It is about finding that balance between doing the best for your customers, whilst honouring what is best for you. This agreement can really help you to stay fit and well and to not get burned out.

One of the best compliments a customer paid me was when they said, 'I love Barefoot Studio, it feels like coming home, in fact I think it is my second home'.

We like to think of Barefoot Studio as a warm and welcoming home. Everyone is welcome and the Studio should feel like a safe place, without judgement, without assumptions, just a happy space.

More and more entrepreneurs are setting up in business where their passion for what they do comes ahead of profits. It is a great way of thinking. People will be able to discern that your business is authentic and not merely driven by profit. Make happiness your business model.

The country of Bhutan measures sustainable development in terms of happiness rather than the traditional GDP measure based on material fulfilment. Measuring Gross National Happiness is all about quality of life, how much leisure time you have, your sense of belonging to a community and how integrated you feel with your culture. As you read through the last part of this book think of as many ways as you can to 'exchange happiness' rather than just cold, hard cash.

In the following Chapters, we are going to explore ways to keep your passion and maintain your own health.

CHAPTER TEN

Be Kind to Yourself

▼

Keep your passion and your health

As time goes by more and more of us in the Health and Fitness industry end up trading our own health and wellbeing for that of our clients. You will never be happy in business if you run yourself into the ground, work 24/7, never take time off, never take holidays and constantly put other people ahead of yourself.

People should look at you and see a shining example of the healthy and well person they want to be. You should absolutely 'walk the talk' and be an inspiration. How do you think this will happen if you are not getting enough sleep, if you look haggard, are grabbing fast food because you don't have time to cook, are using that glass of wine too often just to switch off? You are the biggest asset your business has and you have to prioritise looking after that asset.

We are going to look at how you can do this on a long term and sustainable basis. All you need to do is to follow my *happy business rules* in the following sections.

Switch off - the importance of downtime, business free holidays, Sundays off!

In the MANAGE step, I talked about the importance of office hours. I also firmly believe that chunks of downtime are essential.

My first happy business rule for this is:

> **RULE 1** **You must have one full day a week off which is completely free of business and work.**

This does not mean two half days or taking a morning off, because you are working that evening. This means twenty-four hours of total and absolute 'nothing to do with work'. For me this is nearly always a Sunday, and if for some reason I am working on a Sunday, I keep the Monday free instead.

My second happy business rule is that:

> **RULE 2** **You must take holidays and your holiday must be 100% free of business.**

When I was four, my dad gave up his paid job and set up his own business as an insurance broker. For the first few years his office was in our dining room, so work was everywhere, which drove my mum mad. This was well before the days of email and internet, but I remember that even when we were on holiday my Dad would sneak off to a call box to make 'essential' phone calls. After he opened offices and had staff, he used to ring the office at least once a day when we were on holiday. For a short time after these phone calls you could tell he was distracted and not really 'with' us.

Having run my own business for sixteen years and with all the blessings and curses of modern technology, I can imagine how my Dad would have felt. It is so easy to think, 'I will just check my emails, it will only take five minutes'. What you forget is that for the next two hours you are stewing over the one email you read from an unhappy customer or worrying about the post on Facebook from a competitor, announcing they are opening up just down the road from you.

So, no excuses.

My third happy business rule is:

> **RULE 3**   **Turn your smart phone into a dumb phone on your day off and when you are on holiday**

Turn your mobile phone into a basic phone and camera and ignore all the other communication devices on it. Days off and holidays should be technology free, so no emails, Facebook, internet, etc. I turn the emails off on my phone, delete the Facebook App and don't go anywhere near the internet. At first it feels really tough, but after a while your body and your mind will thank you for it.

There is increasing evidence to suggest that being constantly online and available is detrimental to your health. It can lead to being stressed out, exhausted and perpetually teetering on the brink of a cold, or something worse, because your immune system is being fried.

When your business is 'closed' and it is outside office hours, unplug from technology and engage with your physical surroundings. It will help you to rest your brain and to feel refreshed when the next working day starts.

If you are going to stay good at what you do, focused and enthusiastic, you have to have complete breaks. Some of the most successful business people in the world also relish their leisure time. Look at Richard Branson for example. It is completely healthy and permissible to turn your back on your business for periods of time and to enjoy your family, friends and the things you love to do.

Be true to your values and value yourself

If you constantly put yourself second in everything you do, you will get burnt out. I am sure you had some pretty strong values when you started out in business. Maybe you wanted to help people regain their health. Perhaps you wanted to calm people's minds and reduce their anxiety. Perhaps you wanted to help them get them fitter. What if, by running your business you end up making yourself unhealthy, stressed, anxious and unfit?

I want you to go back to the list you drew up about *why you love what you do and why you know it works.* Then ask yourself, when was the last time I had a _____
(fill in the treatment or service you offer) from another Health and Fitness professional? If you are an Osteopath when was the last time you had a treatment from a colleague? If you are a Pilates Teacher when did you last have a lesson with another teacher? If you are a Reflexologist, when did you last enjoy a reflexology treatment?

When you have been teaching Pilates or Yoga all day or working hard massaging clients, the last thing we feel like doing is working on ourselves. I meet so many Pilates Teachers who teach like mad but have stopped doing Pilates themselves. This is really sad.

A real danger of turning your hobby or passion into your job is that you actually stop doing the thing you loved. It is vital that you regularly take your own medicine.

My best friend is a counsellor and when she set up, she explained to me that it is a professional requirement for all counsellors to have a supervisor whom they see monthly. In effect this is the counsellor receiving monthly talking therapy and taking their own medicine. I wish more professional bodies required this of their therapists and practitioners.

In the Health and Fitness industry, we give a lot of ourselves in what we do. We care about the health and fitness of others, we support them to reach their goals, deal with their crises and help them to be the best version of themselves that they can be.

'But what about me?'

Value yourself and ensure that you don't give so much that there is nothing left for you. As well as building in downtime, make sure that you find ways to nurture your own body, mind and spirit. If you have been teaching exercise all week, treat yourself to a massage. If you've been advising people all week on nutrition, then make time to have an evening to yourself where you can cook your favourite food and chill out with friends.

One of the things I love to do is to go for long walks with my dog. I also treat myself to the odd spa day so I can sit in a sauna or jacuzzi and completely wind down. I run, I go for Nordic Walks, I do Pilates. I love to travel and go camping. I book 'Me Time' in my diary and it is as important as the other pressing business tasks in my week.

When I worked in Housing and Homelessness my days were tough. I dealt with some full-on situations and heard people's stories that were really difficult to hear. It was a high pressure environment, often involving crisis management. The easiest and quickest way to switch off when I got home was to grab a beer from the fridge or have a glass of wine. I didn't drink huge quantities but, looking back, alcohol became a speedy way to switch off. When you work for yourself it is easy to fall into the same cycle of behaviour, you get home at nine o'clock at night after teaching classes, eat a late dinner and reach for the wine. Just be mindful if you see this kind of pattern emerging and ask yourself, 'Am I building-in enough time for me? Make sure you keep a hold of the value you placed on being healthy and fit that brought you to start your business in the first place.

So my fourth Happy Business rule for this is:

RULE 4   **Take your own medicine – treat your own body, mind and spirit with the same level of care that you give your clients.**

Ask for help

As your business grows there will be times when it can begin to feel overwhelming.

Here comes the fifth happy business rule:

RULE 5   **When the going gets tough, acknowledge that it's tough and ask for help**

A few years ago, Barefoot Studio moved to bigger premises a little bit out of town. We used to be based on the main street of a busy market town. Most of the businesses were owned by independent traders. We were at one end of the street and the Post Office was at the other end. Walking the length of the High Street to get to the Post Office was usually a pretty social occasion. I would bump into many local business owners and the conversation always went something like this:

Me: 'Hi, how's it all going'

Shop owner: 'Yes brilliant, you know busy, busy'

Me: 'Business good?'

Shop owner: 'Yes really busy, we were rushed off our feet yesterday'

You get the picture. We all knew that everyone was struggling. The recession had just hit and retail had taken a nose dive. Yet we were all guilty of faking the good times, telling other people how marvellous it all was and how busy we were. As long as we were busy, surely we were making some money.

Now, I'm not suggesting that you talk to your customers or clients if you are struggling but do talk to someone and ask for help. You'd be surprised how many people have experienced the issues you are currently facing and are more than happy to help you through them. Turn to another therapist who uses the same treatment rooms as you, or talk to another fitness teacher that you know.

When the businesses in our town recognised that the recession was going to last for a while we started to get together and work in groups to help jointly market our businesses, run cross-promotions etc. We supported each other and we were all stronger as a result.

When you hit a block or problem in your business, if you don't know what to do, turn to other people. It may be that you need to pay and bring in a professional to help resolve the issue. If you are wasting time or losing money because you are unable to resolve the problem on your own, then it will be money well spent. You may not always need a professional. Maybe you need to call an emergency meeting of your Virtual Team or ring up a friend to talk it through.

If you repeatedly come up against the same problem, you need to do three things:

1. Ask for help so you can resolve the immediate problem.

2. Take a moment to reflect on why this issue or problem came to a head at this time. What could you have done differently? What can you do to stop this problem happening again?

3. Put in place a long-term solution. If you are over-stretched it might be time to get more help on a permanent basis, or to arrange for a freelance person to manage the issue that keeps coming up.

Talk this whole process through with someone. It really is true, a problem shared is a problem halved.

In Step 5 of the *Thrive* Model, MANAGE, I talked at length about building a Virtual Team. I want to mention this again as it is an important part of having a sustainable and happy business.

Many people who run a Health and Fitness business don't have a business partner or staff team. They work alone. Not everyone has a supportive partner who is willing to talk through how it is going. If this is you, work can become lonely and isolating. So make sure you make your own Virtual Team. Hook up with other therapists or fitness Instructors and have a weekly Team Meeting. It doesn't matter if you all do different things or even if you are in completely different business fields. Agree an agenda and keep the group to a maximum of six people. For example, if you meet for ninety minutes:

- Spend twenty minutes catching up

- Allocate each member of the group ten minutes to work through a problem with the help of the rest of the group. The member explains their problem for two minutes and then for the remaining eight, the group discusses solutions

♦ Have ten minutes at the end to wrap things up.

Whether you formalise it or not, surround yourself with positive people and role models who can give you advice and support. You don't always have to take other people's advice but the process of talking it through with them will clarify your own thinking.

 **DO! EXERCISE**

Diarise your days off and regular holidays. Follow these five happy business rules to make sure you stay well and that your business thrives and keeps its vitality:

1. You must have one full day a week off which is completely free of business and work.

2. You must take holidays and your holiday must be 100% free of business

3. Turn your smart phone into a dumb phone on your day off and when you are on holiday

4. Take your own medicine – treat your own body, mind and spirit with the same level of care that you give your clients

5. When the going gets tough, acknowledge that it's tough and ask for help

CHAPTER ELEVEN

Pause and Review

▼

It is essential in business to continually reflect on how you are performing as well as looking forward and planning ahead.

At least once a year, sit down for a pause and review of your business. Fix this date in your diary, ideally at a time of year optimum for your business. For example, you might always have your pause and review in November, in time for price changes in January. Alternatively, you might schedule it for just before the end of your Financial Year. Whichever date you choose, put it in your diary and commit to it annually.

I favour an 'away day' approach to a pause and review. You may want to ask someone to facilitate the session for you or it might be something you do with your Virtual Team or Mentor. Getting away from the work place or your home if you work from home helps you focus on the task at hand and gives the occasion a special feel. It is very hard to review your performance on your own so do find someone who can work with you for this session.

Use the 5 Ms as a framework for the review and make sure you take notes. Every year you can refer to the notes and have something against which to measure performance.

Below I set out a suggested framework for your Pause and Review. The principle is to reflect on the last twelve months and set goals for the next twelve months in each of the areas of MINDSET, MAP, MONETISE, MARKET and MANAGE.

Mindset

- How have you found the last twelve months?
- On a scale of one to ten (one being the lowest) how much like a business owner do you feel?
- What do you enjoy most about being in business?
- What keeps you awake at night?

Mapping

- Review your initial targets and goals. How have you performed against these?
- In broad terms only, what are your current income levels compared with your projections?
- Have there been any changes to your Tribe? Has the demographic shifted?
- Are there any emerging new groups of people with whom you would like to work?
- Has anything changed externally for example, new research, new methodologies, changes in general lifestyles or behaviours?
- Set goals for the next twelve months.

Money

◆ Was your rate card for the last twelve months appropriate? In hindsight, did you undercharge or did you get the feeling that you were over charging?

◆ Compare your actual operational costs with your forecasted operational costs.

◆ Review your income, expenditure and profit and loss.

◆ Were there any unforeseen expenditures in the last twelve months?

◆ Are you anticipating any additional one off expenditures in the next twelve months, e.g. buying new equipment, redeveloping your website?

◆ Agree your Rate Card for the next twelve months and include an increase in charges even if it is a small one.

◆ Set income targets for the next twelve months.

Market

◆ How well did your marketing strategy perform over the last 12 months?

◆ What worked well and what was ineffective?

◆ Review the answers that people gave to the question: 'Where did you hear about me from' on your Enrolment Forms. What could you do to capitalise on the top three most common answers?

◆ Are your key messages still relevant and hitting your Tribe? What changes, if any, do you need to make?

◆ Are there any new markets you want to access in the next twelve months?

- Have any partnership opportunities presented themselves which you could explore in the next twelve months?
- Has anything appeared in the press that you could piggyback on, e.g. someone famous endorsing whatever it is that you do or a new report that has raised awareness around an issue, e.g. childhood obesity?

Manage

- What management challenges did you face in the last twelve months?
- What, if anything, would you have done differently?
- How is your work/life balance? Have you stuck to your Office Hours?
- Is any one aspect of managing the business over-whelming you? Do you need to buy in help or expand your Team?
- How much holiday did you have last year? Are you maintaining at least one full business free day a week?
- Do you need to build in more down time?
- Have you had access to the support you've needed in the last twelve months? If not, where can you access more support?

Other problem-solving

Where you have hit problems, or faced challenges, see if you can come up with specific short, medium and long term strategies for resolving these problems.

For example, you may be finding dealing with customer enquiries, phone calls and email increasingly time consuming as you get busier. You may also find that you are not always able to respond to people as quickly as you'd like. You recognise that very soon you are going to need to enlist someone to help with this.

Short term 0-3 months: Ensure that you chunk sections of time daily to deal with all enquiries. Explore IT solutions that would reduce the time you would have to spend on this. Is it possible for clients to book online for example?

Medium term 3-6 months: Cost out and plan to recruit additional staff support.

Long term 6-12 months: Have receptionist in place

Training needs

- Have you identified any skills gaps that need to be plugged with training?
- What continuing professional development requirements do you have in the next year to maintain professional memberships?
- From a personal development point of view, are there any Course(s) or Conferences you would like to attend?
- What are the financial and time implications of any of the above?

Celebrate your successes

Take time at the end of your Pause and Review Day to acknowledge and celebrate your key successes from the last twelve months.

- What was your best business success?
- What was your personal highlight of the year?
- What were the three biggest achievements for you and your business?

If you do a full Pause and Review of your business once a year, there is quite a lot to get through. Do some preparation in advance of the session to make sure that you have all the facts at your fingertips. I would recommend putting a full day aside for an Annual Pause and Review so that you can take your time and be thorough.

Following this you should have a clear set of targets for the next year. These targets should be very specific, measurable and time specific. For example: I will double the number of one to one clients I have by x date. How you perform against these will then set the focus for the next years Pause and Review.

There is something very rewarding about tracking your progress in business. It can be motivating and it will help you to celebrate the highs and learn from the lows.

The following story illustrates this:

We had a Pause and Review Day at Barefoot Studio, which we paid a Business Mentor to facilitate externally. We hired a room in a Conference Centre and myself, my partner and Ruth, the Business Coach attended. Ruth was really good at asking hard hitting questions and also at making us be 'SMART'[1] with our goal setting for the following year. We were discussing a new project which would involve expanding into

---

1   S.M.A.R.T goals are Specific, Measurable, Agreed Upon, Realistic and Time Specific

a new area of business. I expressed a concern I had about my personal capacity to take on much more commitment. Ruth asked me to be more specific. As I reflected, I realised I was teaching way too many hours of group classes and private reformer sessions. I was beginning to feel burnt out. I said something vague like I'd like to teach less. Ruth drilled down and made me be more specific. We agreed exactly how many hours of group classes and how many private sessions I would be teaching in the future and that this would be in place within six months. It was roughly half what I was currently teaching. Part of the plan was to recruit more teachers to fill the void as my teaching hours reduced. It sounded very nice, working two evenings a week instead of four, chunking my time so I had two completely teaching free days a week to focus on other aspects of the business. I was not convinced it would work but at least we had a plan and a goal. Fast forward a year to our Pause and Review Day. We started by looking back at the notes from the previous year and the targets we'd set for my teaching hours. A year on and I'd been working my reduced teaching hours for about seven months. It felt great that we'd made it happen and that the business had continued to increase its profitability despite my reduced hours.

If you don't set the intention and then work towards it, you will meander all over the place, like someone wandering through a maze. You may be lucky and stumble across the fountain at the centre of the maze but you are much more likely to get there if you have a clear mindset, road map and timescale.

CHAPTER TWELVE

Do!

▼

Just get started!

I know you may not have had time to implement all the suggestions that are in this book but I hope that by reading through the *Thrive* Model, your attitude to running your Health and Fitness business will have started to shift.

In the first part of this book I asked you to consider five questions. I've reframed the questions so instead of reflecting on what you may have done previously, I want you to think about how you will work in the future.

1. Will you work with someone free of charge because their story affects you and it feels 'wrong' to charge?

2. Will you allow people to late cancel their appointments without charging them because you feel it is not their fault that they were in pain or that they were struggling on that day?

3. Will you decide what to charge based on what you think people should/could pay rather than what would be profitable and fair for you?

4. Will you work reactively rather than with a clear plan for what you need to earn or with goals and targets?

5. Will you spend as little time as possible on the business side of what you do _ fire fighting, rather than working to a plan?

I really hope that your business mindset has begun to change and that you recognise the value of what you do. The *Thrive* model is a simple set of steps you can follow. It gives you a framework to plan your business around and against which to measure your progress. You should be able to break down the running of your business into manageable chunks and to find a way that makes it enjoyable.

Use and reuse the **DO! EXERCISES** and delve into the chapters as and when you need. I hope you will keep this book for reference so that you can refer to it time and again.

I want you to believe that you can do it. That you can run a successful, profitable and happy, Health and Fitness business. This book is full of the tools that you need and ideas and suggestions for where you can find extra resources and support. You are good at what you do. You already know a great deal about your field of Health and Fitness. I bet that if I could engage you right now in a conversation about 'your thing' you'd be animated, enthused and passionate. I want you to harness some of that enthusiasm and passion and use it on your journey to becoming a successful business person.

Owning your own business and supporting yourself financially is an incredibly rewarding experience. In time, you'll find that the very tasks that once scared you are actually enjoyable. You will realise how far you have come on your journey when you find yourself giving help and advice to someone else who is just starting out as you once did.

Setting up Barefoot Studio and running my own business for the last sixteen years has been one of the most rewarding times of my life. I'm immensely proud of what I've achieved. Over the years, I have honed my approach to running a Health and Fitness business and I've distilled as much of that knowledge as I can into this book. I hope that the *Thrive* model I have developed helps you to avoid some of the mistakes I've made and that it will make your journey an enjoyable one.

I want to share a true story which illustrates the philosophy behind this book.

I live in a cottage where there is no mains gas. I run the heating and hot water on wood. We get through tonnes and tonnes of logs a year.

One year I decided that I would be able to get a much better price for logs if I calculated what I'd need for an entire winter and ordered it all in one go. I did the calculation, rang around, got the best price and then booked a delivery. I wasn't in when the logs were delivered. I'd told the company to dump them on the drive and, if necessary, on the front garden.

On delivery day, I drove home from work excited at the thought of seeing my winter's worth of beautiful logs. I turned the corner into the lane where I live and the breath went out of me. I could hardly see my house for the mountain of logs outside. They were piled high on the drive, spilled over onto the lawn and were all down the path. I could just about step round them to get to my front door. What had I been thinking?

Now, one small detail about where I live. It is a row of four cottages and I have no immediate rear access to the back garden, where my log stores are located. So I have to wheelbarrow deliveries from the front garden along the small path between me and my neighbour, straight in through the kitchen and then out of the back door, across the decking, down three steps and across the lawn to the log stores on the sunny side of the garden.

I gingerly picked my way around this huge pile of logs, snuck in my back door, put the kettle on and tried to forget that the logs were there. There was no way I was going to move this lot. Where would I even begin? Where was I going to put them all?

For the next week I didn't move one single log, I couldn't face it. I just drove home from work, pretended they weren't there and picked my way through them to the front door. In the morning, I'd happily drive off to work. In my mind, the pile of logs was getting bigger and bigger. It was an impossible mountain.

By the weekend, I realised I had to start somewhere, so I put on my gardening gloves, pumped up the tyre on my wheel-barrow and started, one log at a time. It was hard work. The pile didn't seem to be getting any smaller but at least I was tackling the log mountain head on. Every day I moved just a few more logs.

The following weekend I rang a few mates and offered them a barbeque in exchange for a bit of help. David is really strong, Kit loved filling the wheelbarrows, Vic turned out to be great at steering the full wheelbarrow around the route to the log store, Ceri stacked logs brilliantly and kept spirits up. Paula kept us plied with tea and cakes and made sure no one got hurt! We laughed, we moaned and we had a great party at the end, with me buying the beers to say thank you.

We didn't get the job finished in one day but my support team of friends made it feel possible. I was two thirds of the way down the log pile and I could see how I could manage to get the job finished.

When I placed the final log on the pile in the back garden it was with a huge sense of relief. Like all good business people, as I put a match to my first winter fire later that year, I had a little pause and review. I worked out that I'd saved about £125 on my winter log bill. Was it worth repeating? No! The time it had taken to shift such a mountain of logs in a short time was too much. The whole process was too stressful and I didn't have the capacity to cope. I would never have been able to do it without the help of my friends.

Sometimes, the reality of running a Health and Fitness business can be overwhelming. We may pretend that the business aspect of what we do can just be ignored. We do this even when we know in our heart of hearts that ignoring it will just make it worse. Any task, no matter how daunting, is always far more manageable when you break it down into bite-size chunks. Being clear about where you are now and where you want to be maps out the best route to achieving your goals. The money side of running a business always has to stack up and you should aim to earn a decent living. This doesn't mean, however, that your whole *raison d'être* is money. You can have a value based business that is also profitable. Put happiness at the heart of your business

If you love what you do, communicate that passion impeccably and treat your customers with respect and kindness. Your business will flourish. Above all, grasp your business with both hands and enjoy it. When you look back on all that you have achieved, I promise you will smile.

I wish you a happy and profitable Health and Fitness business.

References

The Tipping Point: How Little Things Can Make a Big Difference,
Malcolm Gladwell, Abacus: New Ed edition (14 February 2002)

The Four Agreements: A Practical Guide to Personal Freedom,
Don Miguel Ruiz, Amber-Allen Publishing (7 July 2011)

Resources

Karen Ingram runs a training academy which offers business
mentoring and support to people in the Health, Fitness
and Wellbeing sector. For more information please visit her
website www.kareningramacademy.co.uk.

Karen would love to hear how this book and her method have
helped people with their businesses. If you would like to share
your story, please email info@kareningramacademy.co.uk

Acknowledgements

Like running a business, writing a book is a team effort and it would not have been possible without the help and support of some special people:

Paula Wooding, my partner and co-founder of Barefoot Studio and the heart of the business.

The 'chat by the fire crowd' from my Wednesday night Advanced Pilates Class, who ended up as a bit of a Focus Group: Charlotte Torres, Lisa Edwards, Annie Middleton, Louise Evans, Elizabeth Raymond, Lyndsey Miller.

The KPI programme, my mentors and publishers Lucy McCarraher and Joe Gregory of Rethink Press, and my Accountability Group Stephen Feeney, Jody Raynsford, Dita Sen-Gupta and Adrian Stone

A massive thank you to my Beta Readers:

Kristin Litton and her red pen!

Charlotte Torres

Rhiannon Kennard

Vicki Coombs

Shirley Ingram

Paul Griffiths

And to Lewys Brown for fact checking the references and statistics in the book.

www.lewysbrown.com

The Author

Karen Ingram is a movement teacher, working with people to train the body the way it was designed to move, in a way that brings joy and energy to all our movements in everyday life.

Karen is an Instructor, Trainer and International Presenter of Pilates and Nordic Walking. She is co-founder of Barefoot Studio, Wales' leading Pilates Studio, and has taught for over sixteen years.

Karen is a Master Instructor for Peak Pilates and a REPs level 4 Lower Back Pain specialist. She has trained in both classical and modern Pilates and originally certified with Body Control Pilates. Karen is passionate about Nordic Walking and is an INWA National Trainer (International Nordic Walking Federation), delivering Instructor courses throughout the UK for British Nordic Walking CIC.

The Karen Ingram Academy combines teacher training with business skills training. Her passion for working to help other people, and her passion for business have come together to enable others to share her success. As a teacher trainer she has certified hundreds of people to become Nordic Walking Instructors and Pilates teachers and over the years has worked with many therapists, including osteopaths, counsellors, nutritionists, massage therapists, to name a few.

Contact details

Karen Ingram Academy Ltd.
Phone: 01446 775772
info@kareningramacademy.co.uk
www.barefootstudio.co.uk
www.kareningramacademy.co.uk

Moving people to believe they can do it!
By teaching them to be great Pilates teachers, to run
successful businesses and to move without pain.

22355046R00100

Printed in Great Britain
by Amazon